History

HiStory

**A Compilation of Scriptures from the Four Gospels
Arranged in Chronological Sequence**

Presented By

Philip Cameron Ministries

His Story

Published By:
Philip Cameron Ministries
P.O. Box 241241
Montgomery, AL 36124-1241

Printed in the United States of America.

Preface

The contents of this volume are compiled from the Scriptures contained in the four gospels of Matthew, Mark, Luke and John. Using *The Living Bible,* a unique rendition of the Scriptures in clear, modern language, passages from the gospels have been selected which, when placed in sequence, give a sense of flow and chronological continuity.

The passages included, we feel, are those which paint the fullest, most descriptive picture of the incidents and parables of Christ recorded by the writers of the gospels. This, at times, is obviously a matter of some subjectivity, but the end result, we pray, will bring blessing and illumination to the reader. As to the sequence in which the passages have been placed, sincere scholars may reach different conclusions than have been made here, and there are certainly no claims of infallibility in this respect as far as this work is concerned.

Although it is not entirely possible to remove every incongruity when combining the works of four separate writers into one continuous narrative, it remains a fascinating journey of the heart to follow the events of the life of Christ in the order in which they appear to have occurred.

It is, of course, as a witnessing tool to those who have not yet discovered the wonder of His love and mercy and the joy of new life in Him, that we pray this work will have its most frequent use. The primary purpose of this volume, then, is to exalt and honor the Lord Jesus Christ, and to assist as best we can those who seek to know more of Him.

NOTES:

His Story is compiled from Scriptures contained in *The Book*, a special edition of *The Living Bible*. *The Book*, unlike other editions of *The Living Bible*, contains no explanatory footnotes. Material enclosed in brackets is not explicitly stated in the Greek and Hebrew manuscripts of the Bible but is implied in the context and is added to clarify the meaning of the text.

In the passages used in *His Story*, occasional material has also been included by the compiler to promote continuity. Such material is clearly identified within braces {as in this example}.

ACKNOWLEDGEMENT:

Philip Cameron Ministries wishes to express its appreciation for the special assistance rendered by Brian Paterson in the preparation of this book.

Introduction

The breath of God blew gently, and the first man that had ever been, stirred to life. In a garden, set like a precious jewel among the awakening wonders of a brand new world, God and man became friends.

In this garden paradise, nothing was lacking. Adam and Eve lived in the midst of majestic, perfect beauty; everything they could ever need or wish for surrounded them in abundance. Then, when everything should have been so right, it all began to go horribly wrong. Man decided he knew better than God, and he disobeyed his own Creator.

Sin descended like a vast curtain of despair, standing between a Holy God and those He loved so much. There was no way man could ever undo what he had done, no way to bridge the gulf he himself had created. Mankind was doomed to spend eternity cut off from God, with no remedy — at least that's what the serpent thought. But in the very garden where that senseless rebellion had taken place, God declared that He would be the one to make a way back. He would send someone to crush the serpent's head **(Genesis 3:15)**, someone who would defeat Satan's evil plans for man, and restore the precious fellowship that sin had destroyed.

That was just the first of God's promises; many more would follow over the next 4,000 years or so. One day, a Savior would come. He would make a way for man. He would pay the price for sin with His own life. The punishment due to mankind would be meted out to Him instead. Who would this Savior be? Who could accomplish such a thing as this? Whom would God send?

7

God would send His own Son, the perfect, sinless Lamb of God, for He was the only one whose sacrifice would be sufficient to dispel the awful burden of sin.

God chose the nation of Israel as His own special people, the ones through whom He would send His Son. Israel's prophets spoke throughout the centuries, pointing the way ahead to the coming Messiah. They declared where he would be born **(Micah 5:2)**; they told which Israelite tribe he would be born among **(Genesis 49:10)**; they said there would be a messenger to go before Him **(Isaiah 40:3)**; they foretold the method of His death **(Psalm 22:16)**; they even predicted that He would be betrayed by a friend, and what price His betrayer would be paid **(Psalm 49:1, Zechariah 11:12)**. Many more promises were made concerning Him — each one would be uncannily fulfilled.

Time passed and the prophets grew strangely silent. Nothing more was said about the Savior, or when and where he would come. Ten years became twenty, twenty became fifty, fifty became a hundred, and still no word of the Messiah. Two hundred years passed, then three, then four hundred years — still no word! Godly men and women throughout Israel must have wondered, "Did we misunderstand? Were we wrong about the Messiah?" Israel fell under the heel of the oppressors from Rome, and still they heard nothing. The sick, the blind, the deaf, the crippled and the poor were all without hope or help.

Then a certain stirring began to take place in Israel. An old man named Simeon is praying in Jerusalem, when the Holy Spirit overshadows his heart and he is promised that he won't die till he sees the Messiah with his own eyes. In the East, some astrologers begin to follow a strange star in the night sky, knowing that some event of awesome magnitude is about to take place.

Then, not in a great palace or in the sumptuous home of some rich aristocrat, but in the simple surroundings of a musty stable, the Son of God took the form of a helpless infant, beginning a life that would alter forever the course of human history.

This, then, is His Story. In the following pages are the words of those who walked with Him. Through their eyes, see the Light shining in the darkness that was their world. Follow Him on the dusty roads of Galilee as he walked into the lives of the sick and the despised, and changed them completely. See the joy on the faces of blind men whose sight returned at His touch. Marvel with the soldier who saw him die, and could only say, "Truly, this was the Son of God." Rejoice with the disciples as they realize that He is no longer dead but forever alive.

This story—His story—is far from over. To men and women everywhere, He still offers eternal life and an answer for sin. In His own words, He gave an invitation that is still open: "Come to me, all *you* who labor and are heavy laden, and I will give you rest." **(Matthew 11:28.)***

Whether this book is your introduction to Him, or is a means to help you know and love Him more, it is a story that will grip your heart. From His conception and birth, to His death, resurrection and ascension, there is no greater story than His Story!

*New King James Version

Chapter 1

A Light Shining Through the Darkness

[1]Before anything else existed, there was Christ, with God. He has always been alive and is himself God. [3]He created everything there is — nothing exists that he didn't make. [4]Eternal life is in him, and this life gives light to all mankind. [5]His life is the light that shines through the darkness — and the darkness can never extinguish it.

[6,7]God sent John the Baptist as a witness to the fact that Jesus Christ is the true Light. [8]John himself was not the Light; he was only a witness to identify it.

[9]Later on, the one who is the true Light arrived to shine on everyone coming into the world.

LUKE 1

Gabriel Foretells the Birth of John the Baptist

[5]{There was} ...a Jewish priest, Zacharias, who lived when Herod was king of Judea. Zacharias was a member of the Abijah division of the Temple service corps. (His wife Elizabeth was, like himself, a member of the priest tribe of the Jews, a descendant of Aaron.) [6]Zacharias and Elizabeth were godly folk, careful to obey all of God's laws in spirit as well as in letter. [7]But they had no children, for Elizabeth was barren; and now they were both very old.

His Story

[8,9]One day as Zacharias was going about his work in the Temple — for his division was on duty that week — the honor fell to him by lot to enter the inner sanctuary and burn incense before the Lord. [10]Meanwhile, a great crowd stood outside in the Temple court, praying as they always did during that part of the service when the incense was being burned.

[11,12]Zacharias was in the sanctuary when suddenly an angel appeared, standing to the right of the altar of incense! Zacharias was startled and terrified.

[13]But the angel said, "Don't be afraid, Zacharias! For I have come to tell you that God has heard your prayer, and your wife Elizabeth will bear you a son! And you are to name him John. [14]You will both have great joy and gladness at his birth, and many will rejoice with you. [15]For he will be one of the Lord's great men. He must never touch wine or hard liquor — and he will be filled with the Holy Spirit, even from before his birth! [16]And he will persuade many a Jew to turn to the Lord his God. [17]He will be a man of rugged spirit and power like Elijah, the prophet of old; and he will precede the coming of the Messiah, preparing the people for his arrival. He will soften adult hearts to become like little children's, and will change disobedient minds to the wisdom of the faith."

[18]Zacharias said to the angel, "But this is impossible! I'm an old man now, and my wife is also well along in years."

[19]Then the angel said, "I am Gabriel! I stand in the very presence of God. It was he who sent me to you with this good news! [20]And now, because you haven't believed me, you are to be stricken silent, unable to speak until the child is born. For my words will certainly come true at the proper time."

²¹Meanwhile the crowds outside were waiting for Zacharias to appear and wondered why he was taking so long. ²²When he finally came out, he couldn't speak to them, and they realized from his gestures that he must have seen a vision in the Temple. ²³He stayed on at the Temple for the remaining days of his Temple duties and then returned home. ²⁴Soon afterwards Elizabeth his wife became pregnant and went into seclusion for five months.

²⁵"How kind the Lord is," she exclaimed, "to take away my disgrace of having no children!"

The Birth of Jesus Foretold

²⁶The following month God sent the angel Gabriel to Nazareth, a village in Galilee, ²⁷to a virgin, Mary, engaged to be married to a man named Joseph, a descendant of King David.

²⁸Gabriel appeared to her and said, "Congratulations, favored lady! The Lord is with you!"

²⁹Confused and disturbed, Mary tried to think what the angel could mean.

³⁰"Don't be frightened, Mary," the angel told her, "for God has decided to wonderfully bless you! ³¹Very soon now, you will become pregnant and have a baby boy, and you are to name him 'Jesus.' ³²He shall be very great and shall be called the Son of God. And the Lord God shall give him the throne of his ancestor David. ³³And he shall reign over Israel forever; his Kingdom shall never end!"

³⁴Mary asked the angel, "But how can I have a baby? I am a virgin."

³⁵The angel replied, "The Holy Spirit shall come upon you, and the power of God shall overshadow you; so the baby born to you will be utterly holy—the Son of God. ³⁶Furthermore, six months ago your Aunt Elizabeth—'the

barren one,' they called her — became pregnant in her old age! [37]For every promise from God shall surely come true."

[38]Mary said, "I am the Lord's servant, and I am willing to do whatever he wants. May everything you said come true." And then the angel disappeared.

MATT. 1

[18]{And so, while Mary} ...was still a virgin she became pregnant by the Holy Spirit. [19]Then Joseph, her fiancé, being a man of stern principle, decided to break the engagement but to do it quietly, as he didn't want to publicly disgrace her.

[20]As he lay awake considering this, he fell into a dream, and saw an angel standing beside him. "Joseph, son of David," the angel said, "don't hesitate to take Mary as your wife! For the child within her has been conceived by the Holy Spirit. [21]And she will have a Son, and you shall name him Jesus (meaning 'Savior'), for he will save his people from their sins. [22]This will fulfill God's message through his prophets —

> [23]'*Listen! The virgin shall conceive a child!* She shall give birth to a Son, and he shall be called "Emmanuel" (meaning "God is with us").' "

[24]When Joseph awoke, he did as the angel commanded, and brought Mary home to be his wife, [25]but she remained a virgin until her Son was born; and Joseph named him "Jesus."

LUKE 1

Mary Hurries to See Elizabeth

[39,40]A few days later Mary hurried to the highlands of Judea to the town where Zacharias lived, to visit Elizabeth.
[41]At the sound of Mary's greeting, Elizabeth's child leaped within her and she was filled with the Holy Spirit.

⁴²She gave a glad cry and exclaimed to Mary, "You are favored by God above all other women, and your child is destined for God's mightiest praise. ⁴³What an honor this is, that the mother of my Lord should visit me! ⁴⁴When you came in and greeted me, the instant I heard your voice, my baby moved in me for joy! ⁴⁵You believed that God would do what he said; that is why he has given you this wonderful blessing."

⁴⁶Mary responded, "Oh, how I praise the Lord. ⁴⁷How I rejoice in God my Savior! ⁴⁸For he took notice of his lowly servant girl, and now generation after generation forever shall call me blest of God. ⁴⁹For he, the mighty Holy One, has done great things to me. ⁵⁰His mercy goes on from generation to generation, to all who reverence him.

⁵¹"How powerful is his mighty arm! How he scatters the proud and haughty ones! ⁵²He has torn princes from their thrones and exalted the lowly. ⁵³He has satisfied the hungry hearts and sent the rich away with empty hands. ⁵⁴And how he has helped his servant Israel! He has not forgotten his promise to be merciful. ⁵⁵For he promised our fathers— Abraham and his children—to be merciful to them forever."

⁵⁶Mary stayed with Elizabeth about three months and then went back to her own home.

"He Must be Named John"

⁵⁷By now, Elizabeth's waiting was over, for the time had come for the baby to be born—and it was a boy. ⁵⁸The word spread quickly to her neighbors and relatives of how kind the Lord had been to her, and everyone rejoiced.

⁵⁹When the baby was eight days old, all the relatives and friends came for the circumcision ceremony. They all assumed the baby's name would be Zacharias, after his father. ⁶⁰But Elizabeth said, "No! He must be named John!"

[61]"What?" they exclaimed. "There is no one in all your family by that name." [62]So they asked the baby's father, talking to him by gestures.

[63]He motioned for a piece of paper and to everyone's surprise wrote, "His name is *John!*" [64]Instantly Zacharias could speak again, and he began praising God.

[65]Wonder fell upon the whole neighborhood, and the news of what had happened spread through the Judean hills. [66]And everyone who heard about it thought long thoughts and asked, "I wonder what this child will turn out to be? For the hand of the Lord is surely upon him in some special way."

Zacharias Prophesies

[67]Then his father Zacharias was filled with the Holy Spirit and gave this prophecy:

[68]"Praise the Lord, the God of Israel, for he has come to visit his people and has redeemed them. [69]He is sending us a Mighty Savior from the royal line of his servant David, [70]just as he promised through his holy prophets long ago — [71]someone to save us from our enemies, from all who hate us.

[72,73]"He has been merciful to our ancestors, yes, to Abraham himself, by remembering his sacred promise to him, [74]and by granting us the privilege of serving God fearlessly, freed from our enemies, [75]and by making us holy and acceptable, ready to stand in his presence forever.

[76]"And you, my little son, shall be called the prophet of the glorious God, for you will prepare the way for the Messiah. [77]You will tell his people how to find salvation through forgiveness of their sins. [78]All this will be because the mercy of our God is very tender, and heaven's dawn is about to break upon us, [79]to give light to those who sit in darkness and death's shadow, and to guide us to the path of peace."

[80]The little boy greatly loved God and when he grew up he lived out in the lonely wilderness until he began his public ministry to Israel.

Chapter 2

Jesus Is Born in Bethlehem

[1]About this time Caesar Augustus, the Roman Emperor, decreed that a census should be taken throughout the nation. [2](This census was taken when Quirinius was governor of Syria.)

[3]Everyone was required to return to his ancestral home for this registration. [4]And because Joseph was a member of the royal line, he had to go to Bethlehem in Judea, King David's ancient home — journeying there from the Galilean village of Nazareth. [5]He took with him Mary, his fiancée, who was obviously pregnant by this time.

[6]And while they were there, the time came for her baby to be born; [7]and she gave birth to her first child, a son. She wrapped him in a blanket and laid him in a manger, because there was no room for them in the village inn.

The Angels' Announcement to the Shepherds

[8]That night some shepherds were in the fields outside the village, guarding their flocks of sheep. [9]Suddenly an angel appeared among them, and the landscape shone bright with the glory of the Lord. They were badly frightened, [10]but the angel reassured them.

"Don't be afraid!" he said. "I bring you the most joyful news ever announced, and it is for everyone! [11]The Savior —

yes, the Messiah, the Lord — has been born tonight in Bethlehem! [12]How will you recognize him? You will find a baby wrapped in a blanket, lying in a manger!"

[13]Suddenly, the angel was joined by a vast host of others — the armies of heaven — praising God:

[14]"Glory to God in the highest heaven," they sang, "and peace on earth for all those pleasing him."

[15]When this great army of angels had returned again to heaven, the shepherds said to each other, "Come on! Let's go to Bethlehem! Let's see this wonderful thing that has happened, which the Lord has told us about."

[16]They ran to the village and found their way to Mary and Joseph. and there was the baby, lying in the manger. [17]The shepherds told everyone what had happened and what the angel had said to them about this child. [18]All who heard the shepherds' story expressed astonishment, [19]but Mary quietly treasured these things in her heart and often thought about them.

[20]Then the shepherds went back again to their fields and flocks, praising God for the visit of the angels, and because they had seen the child, just as the angel had told them.

MATT. 2

Visitors from Eastern Lands

[1]{Now when} Jesus was born... during the reign of King Herod... some astrologers from eastern lands arrived in Jerusalem, asking, [2]"Where is the newborn King of the Jews? For we have seen his star in far-off eastern lands, and have come to worship him."

[3]King Herod was deeply disturbed by their question, and all Jerusalem was filled with rumors. [4]He called a meeting of the Jewish religious leaders.

"Did the prophets tell us where the Messiah would be born?" he asked.

⁵"Yes, in Bethlehem," they said, "for this is what the prophet Micah wrote:

⁶'O little town of Bethlehem, you are not just an unimportant Judean village, for a Governor shall rise from you to rule my people Israel.' "

⁷Then Herod sent a private message to the astrologers, asking them to come to see him; at this meeting, he found out from them the exact time when they first saw the star. Then he told them, ⁸"Go to Bethlehem and search for the child. And when you find him, come back and tell me so that I can go and worship him too!"

⁹After this interview the astrologers started out again. And look! The star appeared to them again, standing over Bethlehem. ¹⁰Their joy knew no bounds!

¹¹Entering the house where the baby and his mother were, they threw themselves down before him, worshiping. Then they opened their presents and gave him gold, frankincense and myrhh. ¹²But when they returned to their own land, they didn't go through Jerusalem to report to Herod, for God had warned them in a dream to go home another way.

LUKE 2

Jesus Presented to God in the Temple

²¹...At the baby's circumcision ceremony, {eight days after he was born,} he was named Jesus, the name given him by the angel before he was even conceived.

²²When the time came for Mary's purification offering at the Temple, as required by the laws of Moses after the birth of a child, his parents took him to Jerusalem to present him to the Lord; ²³for in these laws God had said, "If a

woman's first child is a boy, he shall be dedicated to the Lord."

[24]At that time Jesus' parents also offered their sacrifice for purification — "either a pair of turtledoves or two young pigeons" was the legal requirement. [25]That day a man named Simeon, a Jerusalem resident, was in the Temple. He was a good man, very devout, filled with the Holy Spirit and constantly expecting the Messiah to come soon. [26]For the Holy Spirit had revealed to him that he would not die until he had seen him — God's anointed King. [27]The Holy Spirit had impelled him to go to the Temple that day; and so, when Mary and Joseph arrived to present the baby Jesus to the Lord in obedience to the law, [28]Simeon was there and took the child in his arms, praising God.

[29,30,31]"Lord," he said, "now I can die content! For I have seen him as you promised me I would. I have seen the Savior you have given to to the world. [32]He is the Light that will shine upon the nations, and he will be the glory of your people Israel!"

[33]Joseph and Mary just stood there, marveling at what was being said about Jesus.

[34,35]Simeon blessed them but then said to Mary, "A sword shall pierce your soul, for this child shall be rejected by many in Israel, and this to their undoing. But he will be the greatest joy of many others. And the deepest thoughts of many hearts shall be revealed."

[36,37]Anna, a prophetess, was also there in the Temple that day. She was the daughter of Phanuel, of the Jewish tribe of Asher, and was very old, for she had been a widow for eighty-four years following seven years of marriage. She never left the Temple but stayed there night and day, worshiping God by praying and often fasting.

³⁸She came along just as Simeon was talking with Mary and Joseph, and she also began thanking God and telling everyone in Jerusalem who had been awaiting the coming of the Savior that the Messiah had finally arrived.

MATT. 2

Herod Murders the Children

¹³{After all these things happened,} ...an angel of the Lord appeared to Joseph in a dream. "Get up and flee to Egypt with the baby and his mother," the angel said, "and stay there until I tell you to return, for King Herod is going to try to kill the child." ¹⁴That same night he left for Egypt with Mary and the baby, ¹⁵and stayed there until King Herod's death. This fulfilled the prophet's prediction,

"I have called my Son from Egypt."

¹⁶Herod was furious when he lerned that the astrologers had disobeyed him. Sending soldiers to Bethlehem, he ordered them to kill every baby boy two years old and under, both in the town and on the nearby farms, for the astrologers had told him the star first appeared to them two years before. ¹⁷This brutal action of Herod's fulfilled the prophecy of Jeremiah,

¹⁸"Screams of anguish come from Ramah,
    Weeping unrestrained;
    Rachel weeping for her children,
    Uncomforted —
    For they are dead."

¹⁹When Herod died, an angel of the Lord appeared in a dream to Joseph in Egypt, and told him, ²⁰"Get up and take the baby and his mother back to Israel, for those who were trying to kill the child are dead."

[21]So he returned immediately to Israel with Jesus and his mother. [22]But on the way he was frightened to learn that the new king was Herod's son, Archelaus. Then, in another dream, he was warned not to go to Judea, so they went to Galilee instead, [23]and lived in Nazareth. This fulfilled the prediction of the prophets concerning the Messiah,

"He shall be called a Nazarene."

LUKE 2

[40]...The child became a strong, robust lad, and was known for wisdom beyond his years; and God poured out his blessings on him.

The Young Jesus in the Temple

[41,42]When Jesus was twelve years old he accompanied his parents to Jerusalem for the annual Passover Festival, which they attended each year. [43]After the celebration was over they started home to Nazareth, but Jesus stayed behind in Jerusalem. His parents didn't miss him the first day, [44]for they assumed he was with friends among the other travelers. But when he didn't show up that evening, they started to look for him among their relatives and friends; [45]and when they couldn't find him, they went back to Jerusalem to search for him there.

[46,47]Three days later they finally discovered him. He was in the Temple, sitting among the teachers of the Law, discussing deep questions with them and amazing everyone with his understanding and answers.

[48]His parents didn't know what to think. "Son!" his mother said to him. "Why have you done this to us? Your father and I have been frantic, searching for you everywhere."

[49]"But why did you need to search?" he asked. "Didn't you realize that I would be here in the Temple, in my

Father's House?" [50]But they didn't understand what he meant.

[51]Then he returned to Nazareth with them and was obedient to them; and his mother stored away all these things in her heart. [52]So Jesus grew both tall and wise, and was loved by God and man.

Chapter 3

John the Baptist Preaches Repentance

[1]In the fifteenth year of the reign of Emperor Tiberius Caesar, a message came from God to John (the son of Zacharias), as he was living out in the deserts. (Pilate was governor over Judea at that time; Herod, over Galilee; his brother Philip, over Iturea and Trachonitis; Lysanius, over Abilene; and Annas and Caiaphas were High Priests.) [3]Then John went from place to place on both sides of the Jordan River, preaching that people should be baptized to show that they had turned to God and away from their sins, in order to be forgiven.

MATT. 3

[4]John's clothing was woven from camel's hair and he wore a leather belt; his food was locusts and wild honey.

LUKE 3

[4]In the words of Isaiah the prophet, John was "a voice shouting from the barren wilderness, 'Prepare a road for the Lord to travel on! Widen the pathway before him! [5]Level the mountains! Fill up the valleys! Straighten the curves! Smooth out the ruts! [6]And then all mankind shall see the Savior sent from God.' "

[7]Here is a sample of John's preaching to the crowds that came for baptism: "You brood of snakes! You are trying to

escape hell without truly turning to God! That is why you want to be baptized! [8]First go and prove by the way you live that you really have repented. And don't think you are safe because you are descendants of Abraham. That isn't enough. God can produce children of Abraham from these desert stones! [9]The axe of his judgement is poised over you, ready to sever your roots and cut you down. Yes, every tree that does not produce good fruit will be chopped down and thrown into the fire."

[10]The crowd replied, "What do you want us to do?"

[11]"If you have two coats," he replied, "give one to the poor. If you have extra food, give it away to those who are hungry."

[12]Even tax collectors — notorious for their corruption — came to be baptized and asked, "How shall we prove to you that we have abandoned our sins?"

[13]"By your honesty," he replied. "Make sure you collect no more taxes than the Roman government requires you to."

[14]"And us," asked some soldiers, "what about us?"

John replied, "Don't extort money by threats and violence; don't accuse anyone of what you know he didn't do; and be content with your pay!"

[15]Everyone was expecting the Messiah to come soon, and eager to know whether or not John was he. This was the question of the hour, and was being discussed everywhere.

[16]John answered the question by saying, "I baptize only with water; but someone is coming soon who has far higher authority than mine; in fact, I am not worthy of being his slave. He will baptize you with fire — with the Holy Spirit. [17]He will separate chaff from grain, and burn up the chaff with eternal fire and store away the grain." [18]He used many

such warnings as he announced the Good News to the people.

Chapter 4

The Geneology of Jesus

[23-38]Jesus was about thirty years old when he began his public ministry.

Jesus was known as the son of Joseph.
Joseph's father was Heli;
Heli's father was Matthat;
Matthat's father was Levi;
Levi's father was Melchi;
Melchi's father was Jannai;
Jannai's father was Joseph;
Joseph's father was Mattathias;
Mattathias' father was Amos;
Amos' father was Nahum;
Nahum's father was Esli;
Esli's father was Naggai;
Naggai's father was Maath;
Maath's father was Mattathias;
Mattathias' father was Semein;
Semein's father was Josech;
Josech's father was Joda;
Joda's father was Joanan;
Joanan's father was Rhesa;
Rhesa's father was Zerubbabel;

Zerubbabel's father was Shealtiel;
Shealtiel's father was Neri;
Neri's father was Melchi;
Melchi's father was Addi;
Addi's father was Cosam;
Cosam's father was Elmadam;
Elmadam's father was Er;
Er's father was Joshua;
Joshua's father was Eliezer;
Eliezer's father was Jorim;
Jorim's father was Matthat;
Matthat's father was Levi;
Levi's father was Simeon;
Simeon's father was Judah;
Judah's father was Joseph;
Joseph's father was Jonam;
Jonam's father was Eliakim;
Eliakim's father was Melea;
Melea's father was Menna;
Menna's father was Mattatha;
Mattatha's father was Nathan;
Nathan's father was David;
Davis's father was Jesse;
Jesse's father was Obed;
Obed's father was Boaz;
Boaz' father was Salmon;
Salmon's father was Nahshon;
Nahshon's father was Amminadab;
Amminadab's father was Admin;
Admin's father was Arni;
Arni's father was Hezron;
Hezron's father was Perez;
Perez' father was Judah;

His Story

> Judah's father was Jacob;
> Jacob's father was Isaac;
> Isaac's father was Abraham;
> Abraham's father was Terah;
> Terah's father was Nahor;
> Nahor's father was Serug;
> Serug's father was Reu;
> Reu's father was Peleg;
> Peleg's father was Eber;
> Eber's father was Shelah;
> Shelah's father was Cainan;
> Cainan's father was Arphaxad;
> Arphaxad's father was Shem;
> Shem's father was Noah;
> Noah's father was Lamech;
> Lamech's father was Methuselah;
> Methuselah's father was Enoch;
> Enoch's father was Jared;
> Jared's father was Mahaleel;
> Mahaleel's father was Cainan;
> Cainan's father was Enos;
> Enos' father was Seth;
> Seth's father was Adam;
> Adam's father was God.

MATT. 3

Jesus is Baptized

[13]Then Jesus went from Galilee to the Jordan River to be baptized there by John. [14]John didn't want to do it.

"This isn't proper," he said. "I am the one who needs to be baptized by you."

[15]But Jesus said, "Please do it, for I must do all that is right." So then John baptized him.

¹⁶After his baptism, as soon as Jesus came up out of the water, the heavens were opened to him and he saw the Spirit of God coming down in the form of a dove. ¹⁷And a voice from heaven said, "This is my beloved Son, and I am wonderfully pleased with him."

MATT. 4

Jesus is Tempted by the Devil

¹Then Jesus was led out into the wilderness by the Holy Spirit, to be tempted there by Satan. ²For forty days and forty nights he ate nothing and became very hungry. ³Then Satan tempted him to get food by changing stones into loaves of bread.

"It will prove you are the son of God," he said.

⁴But Jesus told him, "No! For the Scriptures tell us that bread won't feed men's souls: obedience to every word of God is what we need."

⁵Then Satan took him to Jerusalem to the roof of the Temple. ⁶"Jump off," he said, "and prove you are the Son of God; for the Scriptures declare, 'God will send his angels to keep you from harm,' . . . they will prevent you from smashing on the rocks below."

⁷Jesus retorted, "It also says not to put the Lord your God to a foolish test!"

⁸Next Satan took him to the peak of a very high mountain and showed him the nations of the world and all their glory. ⁹"I'll give it all to you," he said, "if you will only kneel and worship me."

¹⁰"Get out of here, Satan," Jesus told him. "The Scriptures say, 'Worship only the Lord God. Obey only him.' "

¹¹Then Satan went away, and the angels came and cared for Jesus.

JOHN 1

John Testifies that Jesus is the Son of God

[19]The Jewish leaders sent priests and assistant priests from Jerusalem to ask John whether he claimed to be the Messiah.

[20]He denied it flatly. "I am not the Christ," he said.

[21]"Well then, who are you?" they asked "Are you Elijah?"

"No," he replied.

"Are you the Prophet?"

"No."

[22]"Then who are you? Tell us so we can give an answer to those who sent us. What do you have to say for yourself?"

[23]He replied, "I am a voice from the barren wilderness, shouting as Isaiah prophesied, 'Get ready for the coming of the Lord!' "

[24,25]Then those who were sent by the Pharisees asked him, "If you aren't the Messiah or Elijah or the Prophet, what right do you have to baptize?"

[26]John told them, "I merely baptize with water, but right here in the crowd is someone you have never met, [27]who will soon begin his ministry among you, and I am not even fit to be his slave."

[28]This incident took place at Bethany, a village on the other side of the Jordan River where John was baptizing.

[29]The next day John saw Jesus coming toward him and said, "Look! There is the Lamb of God who takes away the world's sin! [30]He is the one I was talking about when I said, 'Soon a man far greater than I am is coming, who existed long before me! [31]I didn't know he was the one, but I am here baptizing with water in order to point him out to the nation of Israel."

[32]Then John told about seeing the Holy Spirit in the form of a dove descending from heaven and resting upon Jesus.

[33]"I didn't know he was the one," John said again, "but at the time God sent me to baptize he told me, 'When you see the Holy Sirit descending and resting upon someone — he is the one you are looking for. He is the one who baptizes with the Holy Spirit.' [34]I saw it happen to this man, and I therefore testify that he is the Son of God."

JOHN 1

Jesus Chooses His First Disciples

[35]The following day as John was standing with two of his disciples, [36]Jesus walked by. John looked at him intently and then declared, "See! there is the Lamb of God!"

[37]Then John's two disciples turned and followed Jesus.

[38]Jesus looked around and saw them following. "What do you want?" he asked them.

"Sir," they replied, "where do you live?"

[39]"Come and see," he said. So they went with him to the place where he was staying and were with him from about four o' clock that afternoon until the evening. [40](One of these men was Andrew, Simon Peter's brother.)

[41]Andrew then went to find his brother Peter and told him, "We have found the Messiah!" [42]And he brought Peter to meet Jesus.

Jesus looked intently at Peter for a moment and then said, "You are Simon, John's son — but you shall be called Peter, the rock!"

[43]The next day Jesus decided to go to Galilee. He found Philip and told him, "Come with me." [44](Philip was from Bethsaida, Andrew and Peter's home town.)

[45]Philip now went off to look for Nathaniel and told him, "We have found the Messiah! — the very person Moses and

the prophets told about! His name is Jesus, the son of Joseph from Nazareth!"

[46]"Nazareth!" exclaimed Nathaniel, "Can anything good come from there?"

"Just come and see for yourself," Philip declared.

[47]As they approached, Jesus said, "Here comes an honest man—a true son of Israel."

[48]"How do you know what I am like?" Nathaniel demanded.

And Jesus replied, "I could see you under the fig tree before Philip found you."

[49]Nathaniel replied, "Sir, you are the Son of God—the King of Israel."

[50]Jesus asked him, "Do you believe all this just because I told you I had seen you under the fig tree? You will see greater proofs than this. [51]You will even see heaven open and the angels of God coming back and forth to me, the Messiah."

JOHN 2

Jesus Turns Water into Wine

[1]Two days later Jesus' mother was a guest at a wedding in the village of Cana in Galilee, [2]and Jesus and his disciples were invited too. [3]The wine supply ran out during the festivities, and Jesus' mother came to him with the problem.

[4]"I can't help you now," he said. "It isn't yet my time for miracles."

[5]But his mother told the servants, "Do whatever he tells you to do."

[6]Six stone waterpots were standing there; they were used for Jewish ceremonial purposes and held perhaps twenty to thirty gallons each. [7,8]Then Jesus told the servants to fill them to the brim with water. When this was done he said, "Dip some out of it and take it to the master of ceremonies."

⁹When the master of ceremonies tasted the water that was now wine, not knowing where it had come from (though, of course, the servants did), he called the bridegroom over.

¹⁰"This is wonderful stuff!" he said. "You're different from most. Usually a host uses the best wine first, and afterwards, when everyone is full and doesn't care, then he brings out the less expensive brands. But you have kept the best for the last!"

¹¹This miracle at Cana in Galilee was Jesus' first public demonstration of his heaven-sent power. And his disciples believed that he really was the Messiah.

¹²After the wedding he left for Capernaum for a few days with his mother, brothers, and disciples.

Chapter 5

JOHN 2

The Moneychangers Driven Out of the Temple

¹³Then it was time for the annual Jewish Passover celebration, and Jesus went to Jerusalem.

¹⁴In the Temple area he saw merchants selling cattle, sheep, and doves for sacrifices, and moneychangers behind their counters. ¹⁵Jesus made a whip from some ropes and chased them all out, and drove out the sheep and oxen, scattering the moneychangers' coins over the floor and turning over their tables! ¹⁶Then, going over to the men selling doves, he told them, "Get these things out of here. Don't turn my Father's House into a market!"

¹⁷Then his disciples remembered this prophecy from the Scriptures: "Concern for God's house will be my undoing."

¹⁸"What right have you to order them out?" the Jewish leaders demanded. "If you have this authority from God, show us a miracle to prove it."

¹⁹"All right," Jesus replied, "this is the miracle I will do for you: Destroy this sanctuary and in three days I will raise it up!"

²⁰"What!" they exclaimed. "It took forty-six years to build this Temple, and you can do it in three days?" ²¹But by "this sanctuary" he meant his body. ²²After he came back to life again, the disciples remembered his saying this and

realized that what he had quoted from the Scriptures really did refer to him, and had all come true!

²³Because of the miracles he did in Jerusalem at the Passover celebration, many people were convinced that he was the Messiah. ²⁴,²⁵But Jesus didn't trust them, for he knew mankind to the core. No one needed to tell him how changeable human nature is!

JOHN 3

Nicodemus Visits Jesus

¹After dark one night a religious leader named Nicodemus, a member of the sect of the Pharisees, came for an interview with Jesus. "Sir," he said, "we all know that God has sent you to teach us. Your miracles are proof enough of this."

³Jesus replied, "With all the earnestness I possess I tell you this: Unless you are born again, you can never get into the Kingdom of God."

⁴"Born Again!" exclaimed Nicodemus. "What do you mean? How can an old man go back into his mother's womb and be born again?"

⁵Jesus replied, "What I am telling you so earnestly is this: Unless one is born of water and the Spirit, he cannot enter the Kingdom of God. ⁶Men can only reproduce human life, but the Holy Spirit gives new life from heaven; ⁷so don't be surprised at my statement that you must be born again! ⁸Just as you can hear the wind but can't tell where it comes from or where it will go next, so it is with the Spirit. We do not know on whom he will next bestow this life from heaven."

⁹"What do you mean?" Nicodemus asked.

¹⁰,¹¹Jesus replied, "You, a respected Jewish teacher, and yet you don't understand these things? I am telling you what I know and have seen — and yet you won't believe me. ¹²But

if you don't even believe me when I tell you about such things as these that happen here among men, how can you possibly believe if I tell you what is going on in heaven? [13]For only I, the Messiah, have come to earth and will return to heaven again. [14]And as Moses in the wilderness lifted up the bronze image of a serpent on a pole, even so I must be lifted up upon a pole, [15]so that anyone who believes in me will have eternal life.

For God Loved the World So Much

[16]"For God loved the world so much that he gave his only Son so that anyone who believes in him shall not perish but have eternal life. [17]God did not send his Son into the world to condemn it, but to save it.

[18]"There is no eternal doom awaiting those who trust him to save them. But those who don't trust him have already been tried and condemned for not believing in the only Son of God. [19]Their sentence is based on this fact: that the Light from heaven came into the world, but they loved their darkness more than the Light, for their deeds were evil. [20]They hated the heavenly Light because they wanted to sin in the darkness. They stayed away from that Light for fear their sins would be exposed and they would be punished. [21]But those doing right come gladly to the Light to let everyone see that they are doing what God wants them to."

"He Must Become Greater... I Must Become Less..."

[22]Afterwards Jesus and his disciples left Jerusalem and stayed for a while in Judea and baptized there.

[23,24]At this time John the Baptist was not yet in prison. He was baptizing at Aenon, near Salim, because there was plenty of water there. [25]One day someone began an argument with John's disciples, telling them that Jesus' baptism

was best. [26]So they came to John and said, "Master, the man you met on the other side of the Jordan River — the one you said was the Messiah — he is baptizing too, and everybody is going over there instead of coming here to us."

[27]John replied, "God in heaven appoints each man's work. [28]My work is to prepare the way for that man so that everyone will go to him. You yourselves know how plainly I told you that I am not the Messiah. I am here to prepare the way for him — that is all. [29]The crowds will naturally go to the main attraction — the bride will go where the bridegroom is! A bridegrooms friends rejoice with him. I am the Bridegroom's friend, and I am filled with joy at his success. [30]He must become greater and greater, and I must become less and less.

One Sent by God

[31]"He has come from heaven and is greater than anyone else. I am of the earth, and my understanding is limited to the things of earth. [32]He tells what he has seen and heard, but how few believe what he tells them! [33,34]Those who believe him discover that God is a fountain of truth. For this one — sent by God — speaks God's words, for God's Spirit is upon him without measure or limit. [35]The Father loves this man because he is his Son, and God has given him everything there is. [36]And all who trust him — God's Son — to save them have eternal life; those who don't believe and obey him shall never see heaven, but the wrath of God remains upon them."

Chapter 6

JOHN 4

The Woman at the Well

¹When the Lord knew that the Pharisees had heard about the greater crowds coming to him than to John to be baptized and to become his disciples — (though Jesus himself didn't baptize them, but his disciples did) — ³he left Judea and returned to the province of Galilee.

⁴He had to go through Samaria on the way, ⁵,⁶and around noon as he approached the village of Sychar, he came to Jacob's Well, located on the parcel of ground Jacob gave to his son Joseph. Jesus was tired from the long walk in the hot sun and sat wearily beside the well.

⁷Soon a Samaritan woman came to draw water, and Jesus asked her for a drink. ⁸He was alone at the time as his disciples had gone into the village to buy some food. ⁹The woman was surprised that a Jew would ask a "despised Samaritan" for anything — usually they wouldn't even speak to them! — and she remarked about this to Jesus.

¹⁰He replied, "If you only knew what a wonderful gift God has for you, and who I am, you would ask me for some *living* water!"

¹¹"But you don't have a rope or a bucket," she said, "and this is a very deep well! Where would you get this living water? ¹²And besides, are you greater than our ancestor

Jacob? How can you offer better water than this which he and his sons and cattle enjoyed?"

[13]Jesus replied that people soon became thirsty again after drinking this water. [14]"But the water I give them," he said, "becomes a perpetual spring within them, watering them forever with eternal life."

[15]"Please, sir," the woman said, "give me some of that water!" Then I'll never be thirsty again and won't have to make this long trip out here every day."

[16]"Go and get your husband," Jesus told her.

[17,18]"But I'm not married," the woman replied.

"All too true! Jesus said. "For you have had five husbands, and you aren't even married to the man you're living with now."

[19]"Sir," the woman said, "you must be a prophet. [20]But say, tell me why is it that you Jews insist that Jerusalem is the only place to worship, while we Samaritans claim it is here [at Mount Gerazim], where our ancestors worshiped?"

[21-24]Jesus replied, "The time is coming, ma'am, when we will no longer be concerned about whether to worship the Father here or in Jerusalem. For it's not *where* we worship that counts, but *how* we worship — is our worship spiritual and real? Do we have the Holy Spirit's help? For God is Spirit, and we must have his help to worship as we should. The Father wants this kind of worship from us. But you Samaritans know so little about him, worshiping blindly, while we Jews know all about him, for salvation comes to the world through the Jews."

[25]The woman said, "Well, at least I know that the Messiah will come — the one they call Christ — and when he does, he will explain everything to us."

[26]Then Jesus told her, "I am the Messiah!"

²⁷Just then his disciples arrived. They were surprised to find him talking to a woman, but none of them asked him why, or what they had been discussing.

^{28,29}Then the woman left her waterpot beside the well and went back to the village and told everyone, "Come and meet a man who told me everything I ever did! Can this be the Messiah?" ³⁰So the people came streaming from the village to see him.

³¹Meanwhile, the disciples were urging Jesus to eat. ³²"No," he said, "I have some food you don't know about.

³³"Who brought it to him?" the disciples asked each other.

³⁴Then Jesus explained: "My nourishment comes from doing the will of God who sent me, and from finishing his work. ³⁵Do you think the work of harvesting will not begin until the summer ends four months from now? Look around you! Vast fields of human souls are ripening all around us, and are ready now for reaping. ³⁶The reapers will be paid good wages and will be gathering eternal souls into the granaries of heaven! What joys await the sower and the reaper, both together! ³⁷For it is true that one sows and someone else reaps. ³⁸I sent you to reap where you didn't sow; others did the work, and you received the harvest."

³⁹Many from the Samaritan village believed he was the Messiah because of the woman's report: "He told me everything I ever did!" ^{40,41}When they came out to see him at the well, they begged him to stay at their village; and he did, for two days, long enough for many of them to believe in him after hearing him. ⁴²Then they said to the woman, "Now we believe because we have heard him ourselves, not just because of what you told us. He is indeed the Savior of the world."

MATT. 4

Jesus Begins His Ministry

[12,13]When Jesus heard that John had been arrested, he left Judea and returned home to Nazareth in Galilee; but soon he moved to Capernaum, beside the lake of Galilee, close to Zebulon and Naphtali. [14]This fulfilled Isaiah's prophecy:

[15,16]"The land of Zebulon and the land of Naphtali, beside the Lake, and the countryside beyond the Jordan River, and upper Galilee where so many foreigners live — there the people who sat in darkness have seen a great Light; they sat in the land of death, and the Light broke through upon them."

[17]From then on, Jesus began to preach, "Turn from sin, and turn to God, for the Kingdom of Heaven is near."

JOHN 4

[46,47]In the course of his journey through Galilee he arrived at the town of Cana, where he had turned the water into wine. While he was there, a man in the city of Capernaum, a government official, whose son was very sick, heard that Jesus had come from Judea and was traveling in Galilee. This man went over to Cana, found Jesus, and begged him to come to Capernaum with him and heal his son, who was now at death's door.

[48]Jesus asked, "Won't any of you believe in me unless I do more and more miracles?"

[49]The official replied, "Sir, please come now before my child dies."

[50]Then Jesus told him, "Go back home. Your son is healed!" And the man believed Jesus and started home. [51]While he was on his way, some of his servants met him

with the news that all was well — his son had recovered. [52]He asked them when the lad had begun to feel better, and they replied, "Yesterday afternoon at about one o' clock his fever suddenly disappeared!" [53]Then the father realized it was the same moment that Jesus had told him, "Your son is healed." And the officer and his entire household believed that Jesus was the Messiah.

[54]This was Jesus' second miracle in Galilee after coming from Judea.

LUKE 4

The Mob at Nazareth Tries to Kill Jesus

[16]When he came to the village of Nazareth, his boyhood home, he went as usual to the synagogue on Saturday, and stood up to read the Scriptures. [17]The book of Isaiah the prophet was handed to him, and he opened it to the place where it says:

[18,19]"The Spirit of the Lord is upon me; he has appointed me to preach Good News to the poor; he has sent me to heal the brokenhearted and to announce that captives shall be released and the blind shall see, that the downtrodden shall be freed from their oppressors, and that God is ready to give blessings to all who come to him."

[20]He closed the book and handed it back to the attendant and sat down while everyone in the synagogue gazed at him intently. [21]Then he added, "These Scriptures came true today!"

[22]All who were there spoke well of him and were amazed by the beautiful words that fell from his lips. "How can this be?" they asked. "Isn't this Joseph's son?"

[23]Then he said, "Probably you will quote me that proverb, 'Physician, heal yourself' — meaning, 'Why don't you do miracles here in your home town like those you did in Capernaum?' [24]But I solemnly declare to you that no

prophet is accepted in his own home town! [25,26]For example, remember how Elijah the prophet used a miracle to help the widow of Zarephath — a foreigner from the land of Sidon. There were many Jewish widows needing help in those days of famine, for there had been no rain for three and one-half years, and hunger stalked the land; yet Elijah was not sent to them. [27]Or think of the prophet Elisha, who healed Naaman, a Syrian, rather than the many Jewish lepers needing help."

[28]These remarks stung them to fury; [29]and jumping up, they mobbed him and took him to the edge of the hill on which the city was built, to push him over the cliff. [30]But he walked away through the crowd and left them.

[31]Then he returned to Capernaum, a city in Galilee, and preached there in the synagogue every Saturday.

Chapter 7

A Miraculous Catch of Fish

¹One day as he was preaching on the shore of Lake Gennesaret, great crowds pressed in on him to listen to the Word of God. ²He noticed two empty boats standing at the water's edge while the fishermen washed their nets. ³Stepping into one of the boats, Jesus asked Simon, its owner, to push out a little into the water, so that he could sit in the boat and speak to the crowds there.

⁴When he had finished speaking, he said to Simon, "Now go out where it is deeper and let down your nets and you will catch a lot of fish!"

⁵"Sir," Simon replied, "we worked hard all last night and didn't catch a thing. But if you say so, we'll try again."

⁶And this time their nets were so full that they began to tear! ⁷A shout for help brought their partners in the other boat and soon both boats were filled with fish and on the verge of sinking

⁸When Simon Peter realized what had happened, he fell to his knees before Jesus and said, "Oh, sir, please leave us — I'm too much of a sinner for you to have around." ⁹For he was awestruck by the size of the catch, as were the others with him, ¹⁰and his partners too — James and John, the sons of Zebedee. Jesus replied, "Don't be afraid! From now on you'll be fishing for the souls of men!"

[11]And as soon as they landed, they left everything and went with him.

MARK 1

A Demon-Possessed Man is Set Free

[21]Jesus and his companions now arrived at the town of Capernaum and on Saturday morning went into the Jewish place of worship — the synagogue — where he preached. [22]The congregation was surprised at his sermon because he spoke as an authority, and didn't try to prove his points by quoting others — quite unlike what they were used to hearing!

[23]A man possessed by a demon was present and began shouting, [24]"Why are you bothering us, Jesus of Nazareth — have you come to destroy us demons? I know who you are — the holy Son of God!"

[25]Jesus curtly commanded the demon to say no more and to come out of the man. [26]At that the evil spirit screamed and convulsed the man violently and left him. [27]Amazement gripped the audience and they began discussing what had happened.

"What sort of new religion is this?" they asked excitedly. "Why, even evil spirits obey his orders!"

[28]The news of what he had done spread quickly through that entire area of Galilee.

Simon's Mother-in-Law is Healed

[29,30]Then, leaving the synagogue, he and his disciples went over to Simon and Andrew's home, where they found Simon's mother-in-law sick in bed with a high fever. They told Jesus about her right away. [31]He went to her bedside, and as he took her by the hand and helped her to sit up, the fever suddenly left, and she got up and prepared dinner for them!

Jesus Heals Many Sick

^{32,33}By sunset the courtyard was filled with the sick and demon-possessed, brought to him for healing; and a huge crowd of people from all over the city of Capernaum gathered outside the door to watch. ³⁴So Jesus healed great numbers of sick folk that evening and ordered many demons to come out of their victims. (But he refused to allow the demons to speak, because they knew who he was.)

Preaching Throughout Galilee

³⁵The next morning he was up long before daybreak and went out alone into the wilderness to pray.

^{36,37}Later, Simon and the others went out to find him, and told him, "Everyone is asking for you."

³⁸But he replied, "We must go on to the other towns as well, and give my message to them too, for that is why I came."

³⁹So he traveled throughout the province of Galilee, preaching in the synagogues and releasing many from the power of demons.

Healing a Leper

⁴⁰Once a leper came and knelt in front of him and begged to be healed. "If you want to, you can make me well again," he pled.

⁴¹And Jesus, moved with pity, touched him and said, "I want to! Be healed!"

⁴² Immediately the leprosy was gone — the man was healed!

^{43,44}Jesus then told him sternly, "Go and be examined immediately by the Jewish priest. Don't stop to speak to anyone along the way. Take along the offering prescribed by Moses for a leper who is healed, so that everyone will have proof that you are well again."

[45]But as the man went on his way he began to shout the good news that he was healed; as a result, such throngs soon surrounded Jesus that he couldn't publicly enter a city anywhere, but had to stay out in the barren wastelands. And people from everywhere came to him there.

LUKE 5

Jesus Heals a Paralyzed Man

[17]One day while he was teaching, some Jewish religious leaders and teachers of the Law were sitting nearby. (It seemed that these men showed up from every village in all Galilee and Judea, as well as from Jerusalem.) And the Lord's healing power was upon him.

[18,19]Then — look! Some men came carrying a paralyzed man on a sleeping mat. They tried to push through the crowd to Jesus but couldn't reach him. So they went up on the roof above him, took off some tiles and lowered the sick man down into the crowd, still on his sleeping mat, right in front of Jesus.

[20]Seeing their faith, Jesus said to the man, "My friend, your sins are forgiven!"

[21]"Who does this fellow think he is?" the Pharisees and teachers of the Law exclaimed among themselves. "This is blasphemy! Who but God can forgive sins?"

[22]Jesus knew what they were thinking, and he replied, "Why is it blasphemy? [23,24]I, the Messiah, have authority on earth to forgive sins. But talk is cheap — anybody could say that. So I'll prove it to you by healing this man," Then, turn-ing to the paralyzed man, he commanded, "Pick up your stretcher and go on home, for you are healed!"

[25]And immediately, as everyone watched, the man jumped to his feet, picked up his mat and went home prais-ing God! [26]Everyone present was gripped with awe and

fear. And they praised God, remarking over and over again, "We have seen strange things today."

MATT. 9

Matthew is Called by Jesus

⁹As Jesus was going on down the road, he saw a tax collector, Matthew, sitting at a tax collection booth. "Come and be my disciple," Jesus said to him, and Matthew jumped up and went along with him.

¹⁰Later, as Jesus and his disciples were eating dinner [at Matthew's house], there were many notorious swindlers there as guests!

¹¹The Pharisees were indignant. "Why does your teacher associate with men like that?"

¹²"Because people who are well don't need a doctor! It's the sick people who do!" was Jesus' reply. ¹³Then he added, "Now go away and learn the meaning of this verse of Scripture,

'It isn't your sacrifices and you gifts I want — I want you to be merciful.'

For I have come to urge sinners, not the self-righteous, back to God."

LUKE 5

The Jews Ask about Fasting

³³Their next complaint was that Jesus' disciples were feasting instead of fasting. "John the Baptist's disciples are constantly going without food, and praying," they declared, "and so do the disciples of the Pharisees. Why are yours wining and dining?"

³⁴Jesus asked, "Do happy men fast? Do wedding guests go hungry while celebrating with the groom? ³⁵But the time

will come when the bridegroom will be killed; then they won't want to eat."

Old and New Garments

[36]Then Jesus used this illustration: "No one tears off a piece of a new garment to make a patch for an old one. Not only will the new garment be ruined, but the old garment will look worse with a new patch on it!

Old and New Wineskins

[37]"And no one puts new wine into old wineskins, for the new wine bursts the old skins, ruining the skins and spilling the wine. [38]New wine must be put into new wineskins. [39]But no one after drinking the old wine seems to want the fresh and the new. 'The old ways are best,' they say."

JOHN 5

A Healing at Bethesda Pool

[1]Afterwards Jesus returned to Jerusalem for one of the Jewish religious holidays. [2]Inside the city, near the Sheep Gate, was Bethesda Pool, with five covered platforms or porches surrounding it. [3]Crowds of sick folks — lame, blind, or with paralyzed limbs — lay on the platforms (waiting for a certain movement of the water, [4]for an angel of the Lord came from time to time and disturbed the water, and the first person to step down into it afterwards was healed).

[5]One of the men lying there had been sick for thirty-eight years. [6]When Jesus saw him and knew how long he had been ill, he asked him, "Would you like to get well?"

[7]"I can't," the sick man said, "for I have no one to help me into the pool at the movement of the water. While I am trying to get there, someone else always gets in ahead of me."

[8]Jesus told him, "Stand up, roll up your sleeping mat and go on home!"

[9]Instantly, the man was healed! He rolled up the mat and began walking!

But it was on the Sabbath when this miracle was done. [10]So the Jewish leaders objected. They said to the man who was cured, "You can't work on the Sabbath! It's illegal to carry that sleeping mat!"

[11]"The man who healed me told me to," was his reply.

[12]"Who said such a thing as that?" they demanded.

[13]The man didn't know, and Jesus had disappeared into the crowd. [14]But afterwards Jesus found him in the Temple and told him, "Now you are well; don't sin as you did before, or something even worse may happen to you."

[15]Then the man went to find the Jewish leaders and told them it was Jesus who had healed him.

[16]So they began harassing Jesus as a Sabbath breaker.

[17]But Jesus replied, "My Father constantly does good, and I'm following his example."

[18]Then the Jewish leaders were all the more eager to kill him because in addition to disobeying their Sabbath laws, he had spoken of God as his Father, thereby making himself equal with God.

Jesus Tells of His Authority from the Father

[19]Jesus replied, "The Son can do nothing by himself. He does only what he sees the Father doing, and in the same way. [20]For the Father loves the Son, and tells him everything he is doing; and the Son will do far more awesome miracles than this man's healing. [21]He will even raise from the dead anyone he wants to, just as the Father does. [22]And the Father leaves all judgement of sin to his Son, [23]so that everyone will honor the Son, just as they honor the Father.

But if you refuse to honor God's Son, whom he sent to you, then you are certainly not honoring the Father.

24"I say emphatically that anyone who listens to my message and believes in God who sent me has eternal life, and will never be damned for his sins, but has already passed out of death into life.

25"And I solemnly declare that the time is coming, in fact, it is here, when the dead shall hear my voice — the voice of the Son of God — and those who listen shall live. 26The Father has life in himself, and has granted his Son to have life in himself, 27and to judge the sins of all mankind because he is the Son of Man. 28Don't be so surprised! Indeed the time is coming when all the dead in their graves shall hear the voice of God's Son, 29and shall rise again — those who have done good, to eternal life; and those who have continued in evil, to judgement.

Miracles Are His Witnesses

30"But I pass no judgement without consulting the Father. I judge as I am told. And my judgement is absolutely fair and just, for it is according to the will of God who sent me and is not merely my own.

31"When I make claims about myself they aren't believed, 32,33but someone else, yes, John the Baptist, is making these claims for me too. You have gone out to listen to his preaching, and I can assure you that all he says about me is true! 34But the truest witness I have is not from a man, though I have reminded you about John's witness so that you will believe in me and be saved. 35John shone brightly for a while, and you benefited and rejoiced, 36but I have a greater witness than John. I refer to the miracles I do; these have been assigned to me by the Father, and they prove that the Father has sent me. 37And the Father himself has also testified about me, though not appearing to you personally, or speaking to you directly. [38]But you are not listening to him, for you refuse to believe me — the one sent to you with God's message.

[39]"You search the Scriptures, for you believe they give you eternal life. And the Scriptures point to me! [40]Yet you won't come to me so that I can give you this life eternal!

[41,42]"Your approval or disapproval means nothing to me, for as I know so well, you don't have God's love within you. [43]I know, because I have come to you representing my Father and you refuse to welcome me, though you readily enough receive those who aren't sent from him, but represen only themselves! [44]No wonder you can't believe! For you gladly honor each other, but you don't care about the honor that comes from the only God!

[45]"Yet it is not I who will accuse you of this to the Father — Moses will! Moses, on whose laws you set your hopes of heaven. [46]For you have refused to believe Moses. He wrote about me, but you refuse to believe him, so you refuse to believe in me. [47]And since you don't believe what he wrote, no wonder you don't believe in me either."

MATT 12

The Pharisees Condemn Him Again

[1]About that time, Jesus was walking one day through some grainfields with his disciples. It was on the Sabbath, the Jewish day worship, and his disciples were hungry; so they began breaking off heads of wheat and eating the grain.

[2]But some Pharisees saw them do it and protested, "Your disciples are breaking the law. They are harvesting on the Sabbath."

[3]But Jesus said to them, "Haven't you ever read what King David did when he and his friends were hungry? [4]He went into the Temple and they ate the special bread permitted to the priests alone. That was breaking the law too.

⁵And haven't you ever read in the law of Moses how the priests on duty in the Temple may work on the Sabbath? ⁶And truly, one is here who is greater than the Temple! ⁷But if you had known the meaning of this Scripture verse, 'I want you to be merciful more than I want your offerings,' you would not have condemned those who aren't guilty! ⁸For I, the Messiah, am master even of the Sabbath"

A Healing on the Sabbath

⁹Then he went over to the synagogue, ¹⁰and noticed there a man with a deformed hand. The Pharisees asked Jesus, "Is it legal to work by healing on the Sabbath day?" (They were, of course, hoping he would say "Yes," so they could arrest him!) ¹¹This was his answer: "If you had just one sheep, and it fell into a well on the Sabbath, would you work to rescue it that day? Of course you would. ¹²And how much more valuable is a person than a sheep! Yes, it is right to do good on the Sabbath." ¹³Then he said to the man, "Stretch out your arm." And as he did, his hand became normal, just like the other one!

¹⁴Then the Pharisees called a meeting to plot Jesus' arrest and death.

Chapter 8

MATT. 4

Jesus Ministers to Enormous Crowds

[23]Jesus traveled all through Galilee teaching in the Jewish Synagogues, everywhere preaching the Good News about the Kingdom of Heaven. And he healed every kind of sickness and disease. [24]The report of his miracles spread far beyond the borders of Galilee so that sick folk were soon coming to be healed from as far away as Syria. And whatever their illness and pain, or if they were possessed by demons, or were insane, or paralyzed — he healed them all. [25]Enormous crowds followed him wherever he went — people from Galilee, and the Ten Cities, and Jerusalem, and from all over Judea, and even from across the Jordan River.

MATT. 12

"My Chosen One"

[15]...He healed all the sick among them, [16]but he cautioned them against spreading the news about his miracles. [17]This fulfilled the prophecy of Isaiah concerning him:

[18]"Look at my Servant.
See my Chosen One.
He is my Beloved, in whom my soul delights.
I will put my Spirit upon him,
And he will judge the nations.

¹⁹He does not fight nor shout;
  He does not raise his voice!
²⁰He does not crush the weak,
  Or quench the smallest hope;
  He will end all conflict with his final victory,
²¹And his name shall be the hope
  Of all the world."

MARK 3

The Crowds Gather By the Sea

^{7,8}...Jesus and his disciples withdrew to the beach, followed by a huge crowd from all over Galilee, Judea, Jerusalem, Idumea, from beyond the Jordan River, and even from as far away as Tyre and Sidon. For the news about his miracles had spread far and wide and vast numbers came to see him for themselves.

⁹He instructed his disciples to bring around a boat and to have it standing ready to rescue him in case he was crowded off the beach. ¹⁰For there had been many healings that day and as a result great numbers of sick people were crowding around him, trying to touch him.

¹¹And whenever those possessed by demons caught sight of him they would fall down before him shrieking, "You are the Son of God!" ¹²But he strictly warned them not to make him known.

LUKE 6

Jesus Names His Twelve Disciples

¹²One day soon afterwards he went out into the mountains to pray, and prayed all night. ¹³At daybreak he called together his followers and chose twelve of them to be the inner circle of his disciples. (They were appointed as his "apostles," or "missionaries.") ^{14,15,16}Here are their names: Simon (he also called him Peter), Andrew (Simon's

brother), James, John, Philip, Bartholomew, Matthew, Thomas, James (the son of Alphaeus), Simon (a member of the Zealots, a subversive political party), Judas (son of James), Judas Iscariot (who later betrayed him).

The Crowds Gather Again

[17,18]When they came down the slopes of the mountain, they stood with Jesus on a large, level area, surrounded by many of his followers who, in turn, were surrounded by the crowds. For people from all over Judea and from Jerusalem and from as far north as the seacoasts of Tyre and Sidon had come to hear him or to be healed. And he cast out many demons. [19]Everyone was trying to touch him, for when they did healing power went out from him and they were cured.

Chapter 9

MATT. 5

The Sermon on the Mount

¹One day as the crowds were gathering, he went up the hillside with his disciples and sat down and taught them there.

³"Humble men are very fortunate!" he told them, "for the Kingdom of Heaven is given to them. ⁴Those who mourn are fortunate! for they shall be comforted. ⁵The meek and lowly are fortunate! for the whole wide world belongs to them.

⁶"Happy are those who long to be just and good, for they shall be completely satisfied. ⁷Happy are the kind and merciful, for they shall be shown mercy. ⁸Happy are those whose hearts are pure, for they shall see God. ⁹Happy are those who strive for peace — they shall be called the sons of God. ¹⁰Happy are those who are persecuted because they are good, for the Kingdom of Heaven is theirs.

¹¹"When you reviled and persecuted and lied about because you are my followers — wonderful! ¹²Be *happy* about it! Be *very glad!* for a *tremendous reward* awaits you up in heaven. And remember, the ancient prophets were persecuted too.

The World's Seasoning

¹³"You are the world's seasoning, to make it tolerable. If you lose your flavor, what will happen to the world? And you yourselves will be thrown out and trampled underfoot as worthless.

The World's Light

¹⁴"You are the world's light — a city on a hill, glowing in the night for all to see. ¹⁵,¹⁶Don't hide your light! Let it shine for all; let your good deeds glow for all to see, so that they will praise your heavenly Father.

About the Law

¹⁷"Don't misunderstand why I have come — it isn't to cancel the laws of Moses and the warnings of the prophets. No, I came to fulfill them, and to make them all come true. ¹⁸With all the earnestness I have I say: Every law in the Book will continue until its purpose is achieved. ¹⁹And so if anyone breaks the least commandment, and teaches others to, he shall be the least in the Kingdom of Heaven. But those who teach God's laws *and obey them* shall be great in the Kingdom of Heaven.

²⁰"But I warn you — unless your goodness is greater than that of the Pharisees and other Jewish leaders, you can't get into the Kingdom of Heaven at all.

About Being Angry

²¹"Under the laws of Moses the rule was, 'If you murder, you must die.' ²²But I have added to that rule, and tell you that if you are only *angry,* even in your own home, you are in danger of judgement! If you call your friend an idiot, you are in danger of being brought before the court. And if you curse him, you are in danger of the fires of hell.

²³"So if you are standing before the altar in the Temple, offering a sacrifice to God, and suddenly remember that a friend has something against you, ²⁴leave your sacrifice there beside the altar and go and apologize and be reconciled to him, and then come and offer your sacrifice to God. ²⁵Come to terms quickly with your enemy before it is too late and he drags you into court and you are thrown into a debtor's cell, ²⁶for you will stay there until you have paid the last penny.

About Adultery

²⁷"The laws of Moses said, 'You shall not commit adultery.' ²⁸But I say: Anyone who even looks at a woman with lust in his eye has already commited adultery with her in his heart. ²⁹So if your eye — even if it is your best eye! — causes you to lust, gouge it out and throw it away. Better for part of you to be destroyed than for all of you to be cast into hell. ³⁰And if your hand — even your right hand — causes you to sin, cut it off and throw it away. Better that than find yourself in hell.

About Divorce

³¹"The law of Moses says, 'If anyone wants to be rid of his wife, he can divorce her merely by giving her a letter of dismissal.' ³²But I say that a man who divorces his wife, except for fornication, causes her to commit adultery if she marries again. And he who marries her commits adultery.

About Vows

³³"Again, the law of Moses says, 'You shall not break your vows to God, but must fulfill them all.' ³⁴But I say: Don't make any vows! And even to say, 'By heavens!' is a sacred vow to God, for the heavens are God's throne. ³⁵And If you say 'By the earth!' it is a sacred vow, for the earth is his footstool. And don't swear 'By Jerusalem!' for

Jerusalem is the sacred capital of the great King. ³⁶Don't even swear 'By my head!' for you can't turn one hair white or black. ³⁷Say just a simple 'Yes, I will' or 'No, I won't.' Your word is enough. To strengthen your promise with a vow shows that something is wrong."

MATT. 5

Love Your Enemies

³⁸"The law of Moses says, 'If a man gouges out another's eye, he must pay with his own eye. If a tooth gets knocked out, knock out the tooth of the one who did it.' ³⁹But I say: Don't resist violence! If you are slapped on one cheek, turn the other too. ⁴⁰If you are ordered to court, and your shirt is taken from you, give your coat too. ⁴¹If the military demand that you carry their gear for a mile, carry it two. ⁴²Give to those who ask, and don't turn away from those who want to borrow.

⁴³"There is a saying, 'Love your *friends* and hate your enemies.' ⁴⁴But I say: Love your *enemies!* Pray for those who *persecute* you! ⁴⁵In that way you will be acting as true sons of your Father in heaven. For he gives his sunlight to both the evil and the good, and sends rain on the just and on the unjust too. ⁴⁶If you love only those who love you, what good is that? Even scoundrels do that much. ⁴⁷If you are friendly only to your friends, how are you different from anyone else? Even the heathen do that. ⁴⁸But you are to be perfect, even as your Father in heaven is perfect."

MATT. 6

The Right Way to Give

¹"Take care! Don't do your good deeds publicly, to be admired, for then you will lose the reward from your Father in heaven. ²When you give a gift to a beggar, don't shout about it as the hypocrites do—blowing trumpets in the

synagogues and streets to call attention to their acts of charity! I tell you in all earnestness, they have earned all the reward they will ever get. [3]But when you do a kindness to someone, do it secretly — don't tell your left hand what your right hand is doing. [4]And your Father who knows all secrets will reward you.

About Prayer

[5]"And now about prayer. When you pray, don't be like the hypocrites who pretend piety by praying publicly on street corners and in the synagogues where everyone can see them. Truly, that is all the reward they will ever get. [6]But when you pray, go away by yourself, all alone, and shut the door behind you and pray to your Father secretly, and your Father, who knows your secrets, will reward you.

[7,8]Don't recite the same prayer over and over as the heathen do, who think prayers are answered only by repeating them again and again. Remember, your Father knows exactly what you need even before you ask him!

[9]"Pray along these lines: 'Our Father in heaven, we honor your holy name. [10]We ask that your Kingdom will come now. May your will be done here on earth, just as it is in heaven. [11]Give us our food again today, as usual, [12]and forgive us our sins, just as we have forgiven those who have sinned against us. [13]Don't bring us into temptation, but deliver us from the Evil One. Amen.' [14,15]Your heavenly Father will forgive you if you forgive those who sin against you; but if *you* refuse to forgive *them, he* will not forgive *you.*

About Fasting

[16]"And now about fasting. When you fast, declining your food for a spiritual purpose, don't do it publicly, as the hypocrites do, who try to look wan and disheveled so people

will feel sorry for them. Truly, that is the only reward they will ever get. [17]But when you fast, put on festive clothing, [18]so that no one will suspect you are hungry, except your Father who knows every secret. And he will reward you.

Store Your Treasures in Heaven

[19]"Don't store up treasures here on earth where they can erode away or may be stolen. [20]Store them up in heaven where they will never lose their value, and are safe from thieves. [21]If your profits are in heaven your heart will be there too.

How to Have Sunshine in Your Soul

[22]"If your eye is pure, there will be sunshine in your soul. [23]But if your eye is clouded with evil thoughts and desires, you are in deep spiritual darkness. And oh, how deep that darkness can be!

Only One Master

[24]"You cannot serve two masters: God and money. For you will hate one and love the other, or else the other way around.

No Need to Worry

[25]"So my counsel is: Don't worry about *things*—food, drink, and clothes. For you already have life and a body—and they are far more important than what to eat and wear. [26]Look at the birds! They don't worry about what to eat—they don't need to sow or reap or store up food—for your heavenly Father feeds them. And you are far more valuable to him than they are. [27]Will all your worries add a single moment to your life?

[28]"And why worry about your clothes? Look at the field lilies! They don't worry about theirs. [29]Yet King Solomon in all his glory was not clothed as beautifully as they. [30]And

if God cares so wonderfully for flowers that are here today and gone tomorrow, won't he more surely care for you, O men of little faith?

[31,32]"So don't worry at all about having enough food and clothing. Why be like the heathen? For they take pride in all these things and are deeply concerned about them. But your heavenly Father already knows perfectly well that you need them, [33]and he will give them to you if you give him first place in your life and live as he wants you to.

[34]"So don't be anxious about tomorrow. God will take care of your tomorrow too. Live one day at a time.

LUKE 6

Don't Criticize

[37]"Never criticize or condemn — or it will all come back on you. Go easy on others; then they will do the same for you. [38]For if you give, you will get! Your gift will return to you in full and overflowing measure, pressed down, shaken together to make room for more, and running over. Whatever measure you use to give — large or small — will be used to measure what is given back to you.

MATT. 7

[3]"And why worry about a speck in the eye of a brother when you have a board in your own? [4]Should you say, 'Friend, let me help you get that speck out of your eye,' when you can't even see because of the board in your own? Hypocrite! [5]First get rid of the board. Then you can see to help your brother.

[6]"Don't give holy things to depraved men. Don't give pearls to swine! They will trample the pearls and turn and attack you.

Asking, Seeking and Knocking

[7]"Ask, and you will be given what you ask for. Seek, and you will find. Knock, and the door will be opened. [8]For everyone who asks, receives. Anyone who seeks, finds. If only you will knock, the door will open. [9]If a child asks his father for a loaf of bread, will he be given a stone instead? [10]If he asks for fish, will he be given a poisonous snake? Of course not! [11]And if you hard-hearted, sinful men know how to give good gifts to your children, won't your Father in heaven even more certainly give good gifts to those who ask him for them?

[12]"Do for others what you want them to do for you. This is the teaching of the laws of Moses in a nutshell.

The Gateway to Life

[13]"Heaven can be entered only through the narrow gate! The highway to hell is broad, and its gate is wide enough for all the multitudes who choose its easy way. [14]But the Gateway to Life is small, and the road is narrow, and only a few ever find it.

A Tree is Identified by Its Fruit

[15]"Beware of false teachers who come disguised as harmless sheep, but are wolves and will tear you apart. [16]You can detect them by the way they act, just as you can identify a tree by its fruit. You need never confuse grapevines with thorn bushes or figs with thistles. [17]Different kinds of fruit trees can quickly be identified by examining their fruit. [18]A variety that produces delicious fruit never produces an inedible kind. And a tree producing an inedible kind can't produce what is good. [19]So the trees having the inedible fruit are chopped down and thrown on the fire. [20]Yes, the way to identify a tree or a person is by the kind of fruit produced.

"You Have Never Been Mine"

²¹"Not all who sound religious are really good people. They may refer to me as 'Lord,' but still won't get to heaven. For the decisive question is whether they obey my Father in heaven. ²²At the Judgement, many will tell me, 'Lord, Lord, we told others about you and used your name to cast out demons and to do many other great miracles.' ²³But I will reply, 'You have never been mine. Go away, for your deeds are evil.'

The Wise Man and the Foolish Man

²⁴"All who listen to my instructions and follow them are wise, like a man who builds his house on solid rock. ²⁵Though the rain comes in torrents, and the floods rise and the storm winds beat against his house, it won't collapse, for it is built on rock.

²⁶"But those who hear my instructions and ignore them are foolish, like a man who builds his house on sand. ²⁷For when the rain and winds come, and storm winds beat against his house, it will fall with a mighty crash." ²⁸The crowds were amazed at Jesus' sermons, ²⁹for he taught as one who had great authority, and not as their Jewish leaders.

Chapter 10

LUKE 7

Jesus Heals a Roman Soldier's Slave

[1]When Jesus had finished his sermon he went back into the city of Capernaum.

[2]Just at that time the highly prized slave of a Roman army captain was sick and near death. [3]When the captain heard about Jesus, he sent some respected Jewish elders to ask him to come and heal his slave. [4]So they began pleading earnestly with Jesus to come with them and help the man. They told him what a wonderful person the captain was.

"If anyone deserves your help, it is he," they said, [5]"for he loves the Jews and even paid personally to build us a synagogue!"

[6,7,8]Jesus went with them; but just before arriving at the house, the captain sent some friends to say, "Sir, don't inconvenience yourself by coming to my home, for I am not worthy of any such honor or even to come and meet you. Just speak a word from where you are, and my servant boy will be healed! I know, because I am under the authority of my superior officers, and I have authority over my men. I only need to say 'Go!' and they go; or 'Come!' and they come; and to my slave, 'Do this or that,' and he does it. So just say, 'Be healed!' and my servant will be well again!"

[9]Jesus was amazed. Turning to the crowd he said, "Never among all the Jews in Israel have I met a man with faith like this."

[10]And when the captain's friends returned to his house, they found the slave completely healed.

A Widow's Son is Brought Back to Life

[11]Not long afterwards Jesus went with his disciples to the village of Nain, with the usual crowd at his heels. [12]A funeral procession was coming out as he approached the village gate. The boy who had died was the only son of his widowed mother, and many mourners from the village were with her.

[13]When the Lord saw her, his heart overflowed with sympathy. "Don't cry!" he said. [14]Then he walked over to the coffin and touched it, and the bearers stopped. "Laddie," he said, "come back to life again."

[15]Then the boy sat up and began to talk to those around him! And Jesus gave him back to his mother.

[16]A great fear swept the crowd, and they exclaimed with praises to God, "A mighty prophet has risen among us," and, "We have seen the hand of God at work today."

[17]The report of what he did that day raced from end to end of Judea and even out across the borders.

John the Baptist Sends Messengers

[18]The disciples of John the Baptist soon heard of all that Jesus was doing. When they told John about it, [19]he sent two of his disciples to ask him, "Are you really the Messiah? Or shall we keep on looking for him?"

[20,21,22]The two disciples found Jesus while he was curing many sick people of their various diseases—healing the lame and the blind and casting out evil spirits. When they asked him John's question, this was his reply: "Go back to John and tell him all you have seen and heard here today:

how those who were blind can see. The lame are walking without a limp. The lepers are completely healed. The deaf can hear again. The dead come back to life. And the poor are hearing the Good News. [23]And tell him, 'Blessed is the one who does not lose his faith in me.' "

[24]After they left, Jesus talked to the crowd about John. "Who is this man you went out into the Judean wilderness to see?" he asked. "Did you find him weak as grass, moved by every breath of wind? [25]Did you find him dressed in expensive clothes? No! Men who live in luxury are found in palaces, not out in the wilderness. [26]But did you find a prophet? Yes! And more than a prophet. [27]He is the one to whom the Scriptures refer when they say, 'Look! I am sending my messenger ahead of you, to prepare the way before you.' [28]In all humanity there is no one greater than John. And yet the least citizen of the Kingdom of God is greater than he.

MATT. 11

[12]"And from the time John the Baptist began preaching and baptizing until now, ardent multitudes have been crowding toward the Kingdom of Heaven, [13]for all the laws and prophets looked forward [to the Messiah]. Then John appeared, [14]and if you are willing to understand what I mean, he is Elijah, the one the prophets said would come [at the time the Kingdom begins]. [15]If ever you were willing to listen, listen now!"

LUKE 7

[29]And all who heard John preach — even the most wicked of them — agreed that God's requirements were right, and they were baptized by him. [30]All, that is, except the Pharisees and teachers of Moses' Law. They rejected God's plan for them and refused John's baptism.

³¹"What can I say about such men?" Jesus asked. "With what shall I compare them?" ³²They are like a group of children who complain to their friends, 'You don't like it if we play "wedding" and you don't like it if we play "funeral" '! ³³For John the Baptist used to go without food and never took a drop of liquor all his life, and you said, 'He must be crazy!' ³⁴But I eat my food and drink my wine, and you say, 'What a glutton Jesus is! And he drinks! And has the lowest sort of friends!' ³⁵But I am sure you can always justify your inconsistencies."

MATT. 11

Judgement Against Unrepentant Cities Foretold

²⁰Then he began to pour out his denunciations against the cities where he had done most of his miracles, because they hadn't turned to God.

²¹"Woe to you, Chorazin, and woe to you, Bethsaida! For if the miracles I did in your streets had been done in wicked Tyre and Sidon their people would have repented long ago in shame and humility. ²²Truly, Tyre and Sidon will be better off on the Judgement Day than you! ²³And Capernaum, though highly honored, shall go down to hell! For if the marvelous miracles I did in you had been done in Sodom, it would still be here today. ²⁴Truly, Sodom will be better off at the Judgement Day than you."

"Come to Me and I Will Give You Rest"

²⁵And Jesus prayed this prayer: "O Father, Lord of heaven and earth, thank you for hiding the truth from those who think themselves so wise, and for revealing it to little children. ²⁶Yes, Father, for it pleased you to do it this way! . . .

²⁷"Everything has been entrusted to me by my Father. Only the Father knows the Son, and the Father is known

only by the Son and by those to whom the Son reveals him.
²⁸Come to me and I will give you rest — all of you who work
so hard beneath a heavy yoke. ²⁹,³⁰Wear my yoke — for it fits
perfectly — and let me teach you; for I am gentle and
humble, and you shall find rest for your souls; for I give you
only light burdens."

LUKE 7

At the House of Simon the Pharisee

³⁶One of the Pharisees asked Jesus to come to his home
for lunch and Jesus accepted the invitation. As they sat
down to eat, ³⁷a woman of the streets — a prostitute — heard
he was there and brought an exquisite flask filled with expensive perfume. ³⁸Going in, she knelt behind him at his
feet, weeping, with her tears falling down upon his feet; and
she wiped them off with her hair and kissed them and
poured the perfume on them.

³⁹When Jesus' host, a Pharisee, saw what was happening
and who the woman was, he said to himself, "This proves
that Jesus is no prophet, for if God had really sent him, he
would know what kind of woman this one is!"

⁴⁰Then Jesus spoke up and answered his thoughts.
"Simon," he said to the Pharisee, "I have something to say
to you."

"All right, Teacher," Simon replied, "go ahead."

⁴¹Then Jesus told him this story: "A man loaned money
to two people — $5,000 to one and $500 to the other. ⁴²But
neither of them could pay him back, so he kindly forgave
them both, letting them keep the money! Which do you suppose loved him most after that?"

⁴³"I suppose the one who had loved him the most,"
Simon answered.

"Correct," Jesus agreed.

⁴⁴Then he turned to the woman and said to Simon, "Look! See this woman kneeling here! When I entered your home, you didn't bother to offer me water to wash the dust from my feet, but she has washed them with her tears and wiped them wih her hair. ⁴⁵You refused me the customary kiss of greeting, but she has kissed my feet again and again from the time I first came in. ⁴⁶You neglected the usual courtesy of olive oil to anoint my head, but she has covered my feet with rare perfume. ⁴⁷Therefore her sins — and they are many — are forgiven, for she loved me much; but one who is forgiven little, shows little love."

⁴⁸And he said to her, "Your sins are forgiven."

⁴⁹Then the men at the table said to themselves, "Who does this man think he is, going around forgiving sins?"

⁵⁰And Jesus said to the woman, "Your faith has saved you; go in peace."

LUKE 8

Some Women Assist Jesus

¹Not long afterwards he began a tour of the cities and villages of Galilee to announce the coming of the Kingdom of God, and took his twelve disciples with him. ²Some women went along, from whom he had cast out demons or whom he had healed; among them were Mary Magdalene (Jesus had cast out seven demons from her), ³Joanna, Chuza's wife (Chuza was King Herod's business manager and was in charge of his palace and domestic affairs), Susanna, and many others who were contributing from their private means to the support of Jesus and his disciples.

MARK 3

²⁰When he returned to the house where he was staying, the crowds began to gather again, and soon it was so full of visitors that he couldn't even find time to eat. ²¹When his

friends heard what was happening they came to try to take him home with them.

"He's out of his mind," they said.

MATT. 12

A Divided Kingdom Cannot Stand

[22]Then a demon-possessed man — he was both blind and unable to talk — was brought to Jesus, and Jesus healed him so that he could both speak and see. [23]The crowd was amazed. "Maybe Jesus is the Messiah!" they exclaimed.

[24]But when the Pharisees heard about the miracle they said, "He can cast out demons because he is Satan, king of devils."

[25]Jesus knew their thoughts and replied, "A divided kingdom ends in ruin. A city or home divided against itself cannot stand. [26]And if Satan is casting out Satan, he is fighting himself, and destroying his own kingdom. [27]And if, as you claim, I am casting out demons by invoking the powers of Satan, then what power do your own people use when they cast them out? Let them answer your accusation! [28]But if I am casting out demons by the Spirit of God, then the Kingdom of God has arrived among you. [29]One cannot rob Satan's kingdom without first binding Satan. Only then can his demons be cast out! [30]Anyone who isn't helping me is harming me.

[31,32]"Even blasphemy against me or any other sin, can be forgiven — all except one: speaking against the Holy Spirit shall never be forgiven, either in this world or in the world to come.

[33]"A tree is identified by its fruit. A tree from a select variety produces good fruit; poor varieties don't. [34]You brood of snakes! How could evil men like you speak what is good and right? For a man's heart determines his speech. [35]A good man's speech reveals the rich treasures within

him. an evil-hearted man is filled with venom, and his speech reveals it. [36]And I tell you this, that you must give account on Judgement Day for every idle word you speak. [37]Your words now reflect your fate then: either you will be justified by them or you will be condemned."

Some Seek Proof through a Miracle

[38]One day some of the Jewish leaders, including some Pharisees, came to Jesus asking him to show them a miracle.

[39,40]But Jesus replied, "Only an evil, faithless nation would ask for further proof; and none will be given except what happened to Jonah the prophet! For as Jonah was in the great fish for three days and three nights, so I, the Messiah, shall be in the heart of the earth three days and three nights.

"A Greater than Solomon is Here"

[41]"The men of Nineveh shall arise against this nation at the judgement and condemn you. For when Jonah preached to them, they repented and turned to God from all their evil ways. And now a greater than Jonah is here — and you refuse to believe him. [42]The Queen of Sheba shall rise against this nation in the judgement, and condemn it; for she came from a distant land to hear the wisdom of Solomon; and now a greater than Solomon is here — and you refuse to believe him.

When an Unclean Spirit Returns

[43,44,45]"This evil nation is like a man possessed by a demon. For if the demon leaves, it goes into the deserts for a while, seeking rest but finding none. Then it says, 'I will return to the man I came from.' So it returns and finds the man's heart clean but empty! Then the demon finds seven other spirits more evil than itself, and all enter the man and live in him. And so he is worse off than before."

MARK 3

"Who Are My Brothers?"

[31,32]Now his mother and brothers arrived at the crowded house where he was teaching, and they sent word for him to come out and talk with them. "Your mother and brothers are outside and want to see you," he was told.

[33]He replied, "Who is my mother? Who are my brothers?" [34]Looking at those around him he said, "These are my mother and brothers! [35]Anyone who does God's will is my brother, and my sister, and my mother."

MARK 4

The Story of the Sower

[1]Once again an immense crowd gathered around him on the beach as he was teaching, so he got into a boat and sat down and talked from there. [2]His usual method of teaching was to tell the people stories. One of them went like this:

[3]"Listen! A farmer decided to sow some grain. As he scattered it across his field, [4]some of it fell on a path, and the birds came and picked it off the hard ground and ate it. [5,6]Some fell on thin soil with underlying rock. It grew up quickly enough, but soon wilted beneath the hot sun and died because the roots had no nourishment in the shallow soil. [7]Other seeds fell among thorns that shot up and crowded the young plants so that they produced no grain. [8]But some of the seeds fell into good soil and yielded thirty times as much as he had planted—some of it even sixty or a hundred times as much! [9]If you have ears, listen!"

[10]Afterwards, when he was alone with the twelve and with his other disciples, they asked him, "What does your story mean?"

[11,12]He replied, "You are permitted to know some truths about the kingdom of God that are hidden to those outside the kingdom:

'Though they see and hear, they will not understand or turn to God, or be forgiven for their sins.'

MATT. 13

[14]"This fulfills the prophecy of Isaiah:

'They hear, but don't understand; they look, but don't see! [15]For their hearts are fat and heavy, and their ears are dull, and they have closed their eyes in sleep, [16]so they won't hear and understand and turn to God again, and let me heal them.'

But blessed are your eyes, for they see; and your ears, for they hear. [17]Many a prophet and godly man has longed to see what you have seen, and hear what you have heard, but couldn't.

MARK 4

[13]But if you can't understand *this* simple illustration, what will you do about all the others I am going to tell?

[14]"The farmer I talked about is anyone who brings God's message to others, trying to plant good seed within their lives. [15]The hard pathway, where some of the seed fell, represents the hard hearts of some of those who hear God's message; Satan comes at once to try to make them forget it. [16]The rocky soil represents the hearts of those who hear the message with joy, [17]but, like young plants in such soil, their roots don't go very deep, and though at first they get along fine, as soon as persecution begins, they wilt.

[18]"The thorny ground represents the hearts of people who listen to the Good News and receive it, [19]but all too

quickly the attractions of this world and the delights of wealth, and the search for success and lure of nice things come in and crowd out God's message from their hearts, so that no crop is produced.

[20]"But the good soil represents the hearts of those who truly accept God's message and produce a plentiful harvest for God — thirty, sixty, or even a hundred times as much as was planted in their hearts."

Let Your Light Shine

[21]Then he asked them, "When someone lights a lamp, does he put a box over it to shut out the light? Of course not! The light couldn't be seen or used. A lamp is placed on a stand to shine and be useful.

[22]"All that is now hidden will someday come to light. [23]If you have ears, listen! [24]And be sure to put into practice what you hear. The more you do this, the more you will understand what I tell you. [25]To him who has shall be given; from him who has not shall be taken away even what he has.

MATT. 13

The Story of the Wheat and the Thistles

[24]"Here is another illustration Jesus used: "The Kingdom of Heaven is like a farmer sowing good seed in his field; [25]but one night as he slept, his enemy came and sowed thistles among the wheat. [26]When the crop began to grow, the thistles grew too.

[27]"The farmer's men came and told him, 'Sir, the field where you planted that choice seed is full of thistles!'

[28]" 'An enemy has done it,' he exclaimed.

" 'Shall we pull out the thistles?' they asked.

[29]" 'No,' he replied. 'You'll hurt the wheat if you do. [30]Let both grow together until the harvest, and I will tell the

reapers to sort out the thistles and burn them, and put the wheat in the barn.' "

MARK 4

The Story of the Growing Wheat

[26]"Here is another story illustrating what the Kingdom of God is like:

"A farmer sowed his field, [27]and went away, and as the days went by, the seeds grew and grew without his help. [28]For the soil made the seeds grow. First a leaf-blade pushed through, and later the wheat-heads formed and finally the grain ripened, [29]and then the farmer came at once with his sickle and harvested it."

The Story of the Mustard Seed

[30]Jesus asked, "How can I describe the Kingdom of God? What story shall I use to illustrate it? [31,32]It is like a tiny mustard seed! Though this is one of the smallest of seeds, yet it grows to become one of the largest of plants, with long branches where birds can build their nests and be sheltered."

MATT. 13

The Story of the Yeast

[33]He also used this example:

"The Kingdom of Heaven can be compared to a woman making bread. She takes a measure of flour and mixes in the yeast until it permeates every part of the dough."

Jesus' Use of Stories

[34,35]Jesus constantly used these illustrations when speaking to the crowds. In fact, because the prophets said that he would use so many, he never spoke to them without at least one illustration. For it had been prophesied, "I will talk in

parables; I will explain mysteries hidden since the beginning of time."

Jesus Explains the Story of the Wheat and the Thistles

[36]Then, leaving the crowds outside, he went into the house. His disciples asked him to explain the illustration of the thistles and the wheat.

[37]"All right," he said. "I am the farmer who sows the choice seed. [38]The field is the world, and the seed represents the people of the Kingdom; the thistles are the people belonging to Satan. [39]The enemy who sowed the thistles among the wheat is the devil; the harvest is the end of the world, and the reapers are the angels.

[40]"Just as in this story the thistles are separated and burned, so shall it be at the end of the world: [41]I will send my angels and they will separate out of the Kingdom every temptation and all who are evil, [42]and throw them into the furnace and burn them. There shall be weeping and gnashing of teeth. [43]Then the godly shall shine as the sun in their Father's Kingdom. Let those with ears, listen!

Hidden Treasure

[44]"The Kingdom of Heaven is like a treasure a man discovered in a field. In his excitement, he sold everything he owned to get enough money to buy the field—and get the treasure, too!

A Pearl of Great Value

[45]"Again, the Kingdom of Heaven is like a pearl merchant on the lookout for choice pearls. [46]He discovered a real bargain—a pearl of great value—and sold everything he owned to purchase it!

The Fisherman's Net

[47,48]"Again, the Kingdom of Heaven can be illustrated by a fisherman—he casts a net into the water and gathers in fish of every kind, valuable and worthless. When the net is full, he drags it up onto the beach and sits down and sorts out the edible ones into crates and throws the others away. [49]That is the way it will be at the end of the world—the angels will come and separate the wicked people from the godly, [50]casting the wicked into the fire; there shall be weeping and gnashing of teeth. [51]Do you understand?"

"Yes," they said, "we do."

Double Treasures

[52]Then he added, "Those experts in Jewish law who are now my disciples have double treasures—from the Old Testament as well as from the New!"

[53,54]When Jesus had finished giving these illustrations, he returned to his home town, Nazareth in Galilee...

Chapter 11

LUKE 8

Calming the Storm

²²One day about that time, as he and his disciples were out in a boat, he suggested that they cross to the other side of the lake.

MARK 4

³⁶So they took him just as he was and started out, leaving the crowds behind (though other boats followed). ³⁷But soon a terrible storm arose. High waves began to break into the boat until it was nearly full of water and about to sink. ³⁸Jesus was asleep at the back of the boat with his head on a cushion. Frantically they wakened him, shouting, "Teacher, don't you even care that we are all about to drown?"

³⁹Then he rebuked the wind and said to the sea, "Quiet down!" And the wind fell, and there was great calm!

⁴⁰And he asked them, "Why were you so fearful? Don't you even yet have confidence in me?"

⁴¹And they were filled with awe and said among themselves, "Who is this man, that even the winds and seas obey him?"

MARK 5

A Demon-possessed man is Healed

When they arrived at the other side of the lake a demon-possessed man ran out from a graveyard, just as Jesus was climbing from the boat.

[3,4]This man lived among the gravestones, and had such strength that whenever he was put into handcuffs and shackles — as he often was — he snapped the handcuffs from his wrists and smashed the shackles and walked away. No one was strong enough to control him. [5]All day long and through the night he would wander among the tombs and in the wild hills, screaming and cutting himself with sharp pieces of stone.

[6]When Jesus was still far out on the water, the man had seen him and had run to meet him, and fell down before him.

[7,8]Then Jesus spoke to the demon within the man and said, "Come out, you evil spirit."

It gave a terrible scream, shrieking, "What are you doing to me, Jesus, Son of the Most High God? For God's sake, don't torture me!"

[9]"What is your name," Jesus asked, and the demon replied, "Legion, for there are many of us here within this man."

[10]Then the demons begged him again and again not to send them to some distant land.

[11]Now as it happened there was a huge herd of hogs rooting around on the hill above the lake. [12]"Send us into those hogs," the demons begged.

[13]And Jesus gave them permission. Then the evil spirits came out of the man and entered the hogs, and the entire herd plunged down the steep hillside into the lake and drowned.

¹⁴The herdsmen fled to the nearby towns and countryside, spreading the news as they ran. Everyone rushed out to see for themselves. ¹⁵And a large crowd soon gathered where Jesus was; but as they saw the man sitting there, fully clothed and perfectly sane, they were frightened. ¹⁶Those who saw what happened were telling everyone about it, ¹⁷and the crowd began pleading with Jesus to go away and leave them alone! ¹⁸So he got back into the boat. The man who had been possessed by the demons begged Jesus to let him go along. ¹⁹But Jesus said no.

"Go home to your friends," he told him, "and tell them what wonderful things God has done for you; and how merciful he has been."

²⁰So the man started off to visit the Ten Towns of that region and began to tell everyone about the great things Jesus had done for him; and they were awestruck by his story.

Jesus Raises Jairus' Daughter and Heals a Woman Who Touches his Garment

²¹When Jesus had gone across by boat to the other side of the lake, a vast crowd gathered around him on the shore.

²²The leader of the local synagogue, whose name was Jairus, came and fell down before him, ²³pleading with him to heal his little daughter.

"She is at the point of death," he said in desperation. "Please come and place your hands on her and make her live."

²⁴Jesus went with him, and the crowd thronged behind. ²⁵In the crowd was a woman who had been sick for twelve years with a hemorrhage. ²⁶She had suffered much from many doctors through the years and had become poor from paying them, and was no better but, in fact, was worse. ²⁷She

had heard all about the wonderful miracles Jesus did, and that is why she came up behind him through the crowd and touched his clothes.

[28]For she thought to herself, "If I can just touch his clothing, I will be healed." [29]And sure enough, as soon as she had touched him, the bleeding stopped and she knew she was well!

[30]Jesus realized at once that healing power had gone out from him, so he turned around in the crowd and asked, "Who touched my clothes?"

[31]His disciples said to him, "All this crowd pressing around you, and you ask who touched you?"

[32]But he kept on looking around to see who it was who had done it. [33]Then the frightened woman, trembling at the realization of what had happened to her, came and fell at his feet and told him what she had done. [34]And he said to her, "Daughter, your faith has made you well; go in peace, healed of your disease."

[35]While he was still talking to her, messengers arrived from Jairus' home with the news that it was too late — his daughter was dead and there was no point in Jesus' coming now. [36]But Jesus ignored their comments and said to Jairus, "Don't be afraid. Just trust me."

[37]Then Jesus halted the crowd and wouldn't let anyone go on with him to Jairus' home except Peter and James and John. [38]When they arrived, Jesus saw that all was in great confusion, with unrestrained weeping and wailing. [39]He went inside and spoke to the people.

"Why all this weeping and commotion?" he asked. "The child isn't dead; she is only asleep!"

[40]They laughed at him in bitter derision, but he told them all to leave, and taking the little girl's father and mother and

his three disciples, he went into the room where she was lying.

^{41,42}Taking her by the hand he said to her, "Get up, little girl!" (She was twelve years old.) And she jumped up and walked around! Her parents just couldn't get over it. ⁴³Jesus instructed them very earnestly not to tell what had happened, and told them to give her something to eat.

MATT. 9

Jesus Heals Two Blind Men

²⁷As Jesus was leaving her home, two blind men followed along behind, shouting, "O Son of King David, have mercy on us."

²⁸They went right into the house where he was staying, and Jesus asked them, "Do you believe I can make you see?"

"Yes, Lord," they told him, "we do."

²⁹Then he touched their eyes and said, "Because of your faith it will happen."

³⁰And suddenly they could see! Jesus sternly warned them not to tell anyone about it, ³¹but instead they spread his fame all over the town.

Jesus Heals a Dumb Man

³²Leaving that place, Jesus met a man who couldn't speak because a demon was inside him. ³³So Jesus cast out the demon, and instantly the man could talk. How the crowds marveled! "Never in all our lives have we seen anything like this," they exclaimed.

³⁴But the Pharisees said, "The reason he can cast out demons is that he is demon-possessed himself—possessed by Satan, the demon king.

MARK 6

The People of Nazareth Reject Jesus Again

[1]Soon afterwards he left that section of the country and returned with his disciples to Nazareth, his home town. [2,3]The next Sabbath he went to the synagogue to teach, and the people were astonished at his wisdom and his miracles becuse he was just a local man like themselves.

"He's no better than we are," they said. "He's just a carpenter, Mary's boy, and a brother of James and Joseph, Judas and Simon. And his sisters live right here among us." And they were offended!

[4]Then Jesus told them, "A prophet is honored everywhere except in his home town and among his relatives and by his own family." [5]And because of their unbelief he couldn't do any mighty miracles among them except to place his hands on a few sick people and heal them. [6]And he could hardly accept the fact that they wouldn't believe in him.

MATT. 9

The Harvest Is So Great

[35]Jesus traveled around through all the cities and villages of that area, teaching in the Jewish synagogues and announcing the Good News about the Kingdom. And wherever he went he healed people of every sort of illness. [36]And what pity he felt for the crowds that came, because their problems were so great and they didn't know what to do or where to go for help. They were like sheep without a shepherd.

[37]"The harvest is so great, and the workers are so few," he told his disciples. [38]"So pray to the one in charge of the harvesting, and ask him to recruit more workers for his harvest fields."

MATT. 10

Jesus Gives His Disciples Authority to Do Great Works

[1]Jesus called his twelve disciples to him, and gave them authority to cast out evil spirits and to heal every kind of sickness and disease.

[2,3,4]Here are the names of his twelve disciples: Simon (also called Peter), Andrew (Peter's brother), James (Zebedee's son), John (James' brother), Philip, Bartholomew, Thomas, Matthew (the tax collector), James (Alphaeus' son), Thaddeus, Simon (a member of "The Zealots," a subversive political party), Judas Iscariot (the one who betrayed him).

Jesus Sends Them Out

[5]Jesus sent them out with these instructions: "Don't go to the Gentiles or the Samaritans, [6]but only to the people of Israel — God's lost sheep. [7]Go and announce to them that the Kingdom of Heaven is near. [8]Heal the sick, raise the dead, cure the lepers, and cast out demons. Give as freely as you have received!

[9]"Don't take any money with you; [10]don't even carry a duffle bag with extra clothes and shoes, or even a walking stick; for those you help should feed and care for you. [11]Whenever you enter a city or village, search for a godly man and stay in his home until you leave for the next town. [12]When you ask permission to stay, be friendly, [13]and if it turns out to be godly home, give it your blessing; if not, keep the blessing. [14]Any city or home that doesn't welcome you — shake off the dust of that place from your feet as you leave. [15]Truly, the wicked cities of Sodom and Gomorrah will be better off at Judgement Day than they.

A Warning to Expect Persecution

[16]"I am sending you out as sheep among wolves. Be as wary as serpents and harmless as doves. [17]But beware! For you will be arrested and tried, and whipped in the synagogues. [18]Yes, and you must stand trial before governors and kings for my sake. This will give you the opportunity to tell them about me, yes, to witness to the world.

[19]"When you are arrested, don't worry about what to say at your trial, for you will be given the right words at the right time. [20]For it won't be you doing the talking — it will be the Spirit of your heavenly Father speaking through you!

[21]"Brother shall betray brother to death, and fathers shall betray their own children. And children shall rise against their parents and cause their deaths. [22]Everyone shall hate you because you belong to me. But all of you who endure to the end shall be saved.

[23]"When you are persecuted in one city, flee to the next! I will return before you have reached them all!

[24]"A student is not greater than his teacher. A servant is not above his master. [25]The student shares his teacher's fate. The servant shares his master's! And since I, the master of the household, have been called 'Satan,' how much more will you!

Fear Only God

[26]But don't be afraid of those who threaten you. For the time is coming when the truth will be revealed: their secret plots will become public information.

[27]"What I tell you now in the gloom, shout abroad when daybreak comes. What I whisper in your ears, proclaim from the housetops!

[28]"Don't be afraid of those who can kill only your bodies — but can't touch your souls! Fear only God who can

destroy both soul and body in hell. [29]Not one sparrow (What do they cost? Two for a penny?) can fall to the ground without your Father knowing it. [30]And the very hairs of your head are all numbered. [31]So don't worry! You are more valuable to him than many sparrows.

[32]"If anyone publicly acknowledges me as his friend, I will openly acknowledge him as my friend before my Father in heaven. [33]But if anyone publicly denies me, I will openly deny him before my Father in heaven.

"Don't Imagine That I Came to Bring Peace"

[34]"Don't imagine that I came to bring peace to the earth! No, rather, a sword. [35]I have come to set a man against his father, and a daughter against her mother, and a daughter-in-law against her mother-in-law — [36]a man's worst enemies will be right in his own home! [37]If you love your father and mother more than you love me, you are not worthy of being mine; or if you love your son or daughter more than me, you are not worthy of being mine. [38]If you refuse to take up your cross and follow me, you are not worthy of being mine.

[39]"If you cling to your life, you will lose it; but if you give it up for me, you will save it.

Sharing the Reward of the Godly

[40]"Those who welcome you are welcoming me. And when they welcome me they are welcoming God who sent me. [41]If you welcome a prophet because he is a man of God, you will be given the same reward a prophet gets. And if you welcome good and godly men because of their godliness, you will be given a reward like theirs.

[42]"And if, as my representatives, you give a cup of cold water to a little child, you will surely be rewarded."

MATT. 11

¹When Jesus had finished giving these instructions to his twelve disciples, he went off preaching in the cities where they were scheduled to go.

MARK 6

John the Baptist's Death

¹⁴King Herod soon heard about Jesus, for his miracles were talked about everywhere. The king thought Jesus was John the Baptist come back to life again. So the people were saying, "No wonder he can do such miracles." ¹⁵Others thought Jesus was Elijah the ancient prophet, now returned to life again; still others claimed he was a new prophet like the great ones of the past.

¹⁶"No," Herod said, "it is John, the man I beheaded. He has come back from the dead."

^{17,18}For Herod had sent soldiers to arrest and imprison John because he kept saying it was wrong for the king to marry Herodias, his brother Philip's wife. ¹⁹Herodias wanted John killed in revenge, but without Herod's approval she was powerless. ²⁰And Herod respected John, knowing that he was a good and holy man, and so he kept him under his protection. Herod was disturbed whenever he talked with John, but even so he liked to listen to him.

²¹Herodias' chance finally came. It was Herod's birthday and he gave a stag party for his palace aides, army officers, and the leading citizens of Galilee. ^{22,23}Then Herodias' daughter came in and danced before them and greatly pleased them all.

"Ask me for anything you like," the king vowed, "even half of my kingdom, and I will give it to you!"

²⁴She went out and consulted her mother, who told her, "Ask for John the Baptist's head!"

²⁵So she hurried back to the king and told him, "I want the head of John the Baptist — right now — on a tray!"

²⁶Then the king was sorry, but he was embarrassed to break his oath in front of his guests. ²⁷So he sent one of his bodyguards to the prison to cut off John's head and bring it to him. The soldier killed John in the prison, ²⁸and brought back his head on a tray, and gave it to the girl and she took it to her mother.

²⁹When John's disciples heard what had happened, they came for his body and buried it in a tomb.

Chapter 12

MARK 6

Feeding the Five Thousand

[30]The apostles now returned to Jesus from their tour and told him all they had done and what they had said to the people they visited.

[31]Then Jesus suggested, "Let's get away from the crowds for a while and rest." For so many people were coming and going that they scarcely had time to eat. [32]So they left by boat for a quieter spot. [33]But many people saw them leaving and ran ahead along the shore and met them as they landed. [34]So the usual vast crowd was there as he stepped from the boat; and he had pity on them because they were like sheep without a shepherd, and he taught them many things they needed to know.

[35,36]Late in the afternoon his disciples came to him and said, "Tell the people to go away to the nearby villages and farms and buy themselves some food, for there is nothing to eat here in this desolate spot, and it is getting late."

[37]But Jesus said, "*You* feed them."

"With what?" they asked. "It would take a fortune to buy food for all this crowd!"

[38]"How much food do we have?" he asked. "Go and find out."

They came back to report that there were five loaves of bread and two fish.

^{39,40}Then Jesus told the crowd to sit down, and soon colorful groups of fifty or a hundred each were sitting on the green grass.

⁴¹He took the five loaves and two fish and looking up to heaven, gave thanks for the food. Breaking the loaves into pieces, he gave some of the bread and fish to each disciple to place before the people. ⁴²And the crowd ate until they could hold no more!

^{43,44}There were about 5,000 men there for that meal, and afterwards twelve basketfuls of scraps were picked up off the grass!

Jesus Walks on the Water

⁴⁵Immediately after this Jesus instructed his disciples to get back into the boat and strike out across the lake to Bethsaida, where he would join them later. He himself would stay and tell the crowds good-bye and get them started home.

MATT. 14

^{23,24}Then afterwards he went up into the hills to pray. Night fell, and out on the lake the disciples were in trouble. For the wind had risen and they were fighting heavy seas.

²⁵About four o' clock in the morning Jesus came to them, walking on the water! ²⁶They screamed in terror, for they thought he was a ghost.

²⁷But Jesus immediately spoke to them, reassuring them. "Don't be afraid!" he said.

²⁸Then Peter called to him: "Sir, if it is really you, tell me to come over to you, walking on the water."

²⁹"All right," the Lord said, "come along!"

So Peter went over the side of the boat and walked on the water toward Jesus. ³⁰But when he looked around at the high waves, he was terrified and began to sink. "Save me, Lord!" he shouted.

[31]Instantly Jesus reached out his hand and rescued him. "O man of little faith," Jesus said. "Why did you doubt me?" [32]And when they had climbed back into the boat, the wind stopped.

[33]The others were awestruck. "You really are the Son of God!" they exclaimed.

MARK 6

[53]When they arrived at Gennesaret on the other side of the lake they moored the boat, [54]and climbed out.

The people standing around there recognized him at once, [55]and ran throughout the whole area to spread the news of his arrival, and began carrying sick folks to him on mats and stretchers. [56]Wherever he went — in villages and cities, and out on the farms — they laid the sick in the market plazas and streets, and begged him to let them at least touch the fringes of his clothes; and as many as touched him were healed.

JOHN 6

The People Look For Jesus

[22,23]The next morning, back across the lake, crowds began gathering on the shore [waiting to see Jesus]. For they knew that he and his disciples had come over together and that the disciples had gone off in their boat, leaving him behind. Several small boats from Tiberias were nearby, [24]so when the people saw that Jesus wasn't there, nor his disciples, they got into the boats and went across to Capernaum to look for him.

"I Am the Bread of Life"

²⁵When they arrived and found him, they said, "Sir, how did you get here?" ²⁶Jesus replied, "The truth of the matter is that you want to be with me because I fed you, not because you believe in me. ²⁷But you shouldn't be so concerned about perishable things like food. No, spend your energy seeking the eternal life that I, the Messiah, can give you. For God the Father has sent me for this very purpose."

²⁸They replied, "What should we do to satisfy God?"

²⁹Jesus told them, "This is the will of God, that you believe in the one he has sent."

^{30,31}They replied, "You must show us more miracles if you want us to believe you are the Messiah. Give us free bread every day, like our fathers had while they journeyed through the wilderness! As the Scriptures say, 'Moses gave them bread from heaven.' "

³²Jesus said, "Moses didn't give it to them. My Father did. And now he offers you true Bread from heaven. ³³The true Bread is a Person — the one sent by God from heaven, and he gives life to the world."

³⁴"Sir," they said, "give us that bread every day of our lives!"

³⁵Jesus replied, "I am the Bread of Life. No one coming to me will ever be hungry again. Those believing in me will never thirst. ³⁶But the trouble is, as I have told you before, you haven't believed even though you have seen me, ³⁷But some will come to me — those the Father has given me — and I will never, never reject them. ³⁸For I have come here from heaven to do the will of God who sent me, not to have my own way. ³⁹And this is the will of God, that I should not lose even one of all those he has given me, but that I should raise them to eternal life at the Last Day. ⁴⁰For it is my Father's will that everyone who sees his Son and believes

on him should have eternal life – that I should raise him at the Last Day."

⁴¹Then the Jews began to murmur against him because he claimed to be the Bread from heaven.

⁴²"What?" they exclaimed. "Why, he is merely Jesus the son of Joseph, whose father and mother we know. What is this he is saying, that he came down from heaven?"

⁴³But Jesus replied, "Don't murmur among yourselves about my saying that. ⁴⁴For no one can come to me unless the Father who sent me draws him to me, and at the Last Day I will cause all such to rise again from the dead. ⁴⁵As it is written in the Scriptures, 'They shall all be taught of God.' Those the Father speaks to, who learn the truth from him, will be attracted to me. ⁴⁶(Not that anyone actually sees the Father, for only I have seen him.)

⁴⁷"How earnestly I tell you this – anyone who believes in me already has eternal life! ⁴⁸⁻⁵¹Yes, I am the Bread of Life! When your fathers in the wilderness ate bread from the skies, they all died. But the Bread from heaven gives eternal life to everyone who eats it. I am that Living Bread that came down out of heaven. Anyone eating this Bread shall live forever; this Bread is my flesh given to redeem humanity."

⁵²Then the Jews began arguing with each other about what he meant. "How can this man give us his flesh to eat?" they asked.

⁵³So Jesus said it again, "With all the earnestness I possess I tell you this: Unless you eat the flesh of the Messiah and drink his blood, you cannot have eternal life within you. ⁵⁴But anyone who does eat my flesh and drink my blood has eternal life, and I will raise him at the Last Day. ⁵⁵For my flesh is the true food, and my blood is the true drink. ⁵⁶Everyone who eats my flesh and drinks my blood is in me,

and I in him. ⁵⁷I live by the power of the living Father who sent me, and in the same way those who partake of me shall live because of me! ⁵⁸I am the true Bread from heaven; and anyone who eats this Bread shall live forever, and not die as your fathers did — although they ate bread from heaven." ⁵⁹(He preached this sermon in the synagogue in Capernaum.)

The Words That give Eternal Life

⁶⁰Even his disciples said, "This is very hard to understand. Who can tell what he means?"

⁶¹Jesus knew within himself that his disciples were complaining and said to them, "Does *this* offend you? ⁶²Then what will you think if you see me, the Messiah, return to heaven again? ⁶³Only the Holy Spirit gives eternal life. Those born only once, with physical birth, will never receive this gift. But now I have told you how to get this true spiritual life. ⁶⁴But some of you don't believe me." (For Jesus knew from the beginning who didn't believe him and knew the one who would betray him.)

⁶⁵And he remarked, "That is what I meant when I said that no one can come to me unless the Father attracts him to me."

⁶⁶At this point many of his disciples turned away and deserted him.

⁶⁷Then Jesus turned to the Twelve and asked, "Are you going too?"

⁶⁸Simon Peter replied, "Master, to whom shall we go? You alone have the words that give eternal life, ⁶⁹and we believe them and know you are the holy Son of God!"

⁷⁰Then Jesus said, "I chose the twelve of you, and one is a devil." ⁷¹He was speaking of Judas, son of Simon Iscariot, one of the Twelve, who would betray him.

MARK 7

Teachings about Inner Purity

¹One day some Jewish religious leaders arrived from Jerusalem to investigate him, ²and noticed that some of his disciples failed to follow the usual Jewish rituals before eating. ³(For the Jews, especially the Pharisees, will never eat until they have sprinkled their arms to the elbows, as required by their ancient traditions. ⁴So when they come home from the market they must always sprinkle themselves in this way before touching any food. This is but one of many examples of laws and regulations they have clung to for centuries, and still follow, such as their ceremony of cleansing for pots, pans and dishes.)

⁵So the religious leaders asked him, "Why don't your disciples follow our age-old customs? For they eat without first performing the washing ceremony."

⁶,⁷Jesus replied, "You bunch of hypocrites! Isaiah the prophet described you very well when he said, 'These people speak very prettily about the Lord but they have no love for him at all. Their worship is a farce, for they claim that God commands the people to obey their petty rules.' How right Isaiah was! ⁸For you ignore God's specific orders and substitute your own traditions. ⁹You are simply rejecting God's laws and trampling them under your feet for the sake of tradition.

¹⁰For instance, Moses gave you this law from God: 'Honor your father and mother.' And he said that anyone who speaks against his father or mother must die. ¹¹But you say it is perfectly all right for a man to disregard his needy parents, telling them, 'Sorry, I can't help you! For I have given to God what I could have given you.' ¹²,¹³And so you break the law of God in order to protect your man-made

tradition. And this is only one example. There are many, many others."

MATT. 15

[10]Then Jesus called to the crowds and said, "Listen to what I say and try to understand. [11]You aren't made unholy by eating non-kosher food! It is what you *say* and *think* that makes you unclean."

[12]Then the disciples came and told him, "You offended the Pharisees by that remark."

[13,14]Jesus replied, "Every plant not planted by my Father shall be rooted up, so ignore them. They are blind guides leading the blind, and both will fall into a ditch."

[15]Then Peter asked Jesus to explain what he meant when he said that people are not defiled by non-kosher food.

[16]"Don't you understand?" Jesus asked him. [17]"Don't you see that anything you eat passes through the digestive tract and out again? [18]But evil words come from an evil heart, and defile the man who says them. [19]For from the heart come evil thoughts, murder, adultery, fornication, theft, lying and slander. [20]These are what defile; but there is no spiritual defilement from eating without first going through the ritual of ceremonial handwashing!"

Chapter 13

MATT. 15

A Gentile Woman's Faith

²¹Jesus then left that part of the country and walked the fifty miles to Tyre and Sidon.

²²A woman from Canaan who was living there came to him, pleading, "Have mercy on me, O Lord, King David's Son! For my daughter has a demon within her, and it torments her constantly."

²³But Jesus gave her no reply—not even a word. Then his disciples urged him to send her away. "Tell her to get going," they said, "for she is bothering us with all her begging."

²⁴Then he said to the woman, "I was sent to help the Jews—the lost sheep of Israel—not the Gentiles."

²⁵But she came and worshiped him and pled again, "Sir, help me!"

²⁶"It doesn't seem right to take bread from the children and throw it to the dogs," he said.

²⁷"Yes, it is!" she replied, "for even the puppies beneath the table are permitted to eat the crumbs that fall."

²⁸"Woman," Jesus told her, "your faith is large, and your request is granted." And her daughter was healed right then.

His Story

Jesus Heals All the Sick

²⁹Jesus now returned to the Sea of Galilee, and climbed a hill and sat there. ³⁰And a vast crowd brought their lame, blind, maimed, and those who couldn't speak, and many others, and laid them before Jesus, and he healed them all. ³¹What a spectacle it was! Those who hadn't been able to say a word before were talking excitedly, and those with missing arms and legs had new ones; the crippled were walking and jumping around, and those who had been blind were gazing about them! The crowds just marveled, and praised the God of Israel.

MARK 7

³²A deaf man with a speech impediment was brought to him, and everyone begged Jesus to lay his hands on the man and heal him.

³³Jesus led him away from the crowd and put his fingers into the man's ears, then spat and touched the man's tongue with the spittle. ³⁴Then, looking up to heaven, he sighed and commanded, "Open!" ³⁵Instantly the man could hear perfectly and speak plainly!

³⁶Jesus told the crowd not to spread the news, but the more he forbade them, the more they made it known, ³⁷for they were overcome with utter amazement. Again and again they said, "Everything he does is wonderful; he even corrects deafness and stammering!"

MARK 8

Jesus Feeds Four Thousand

¹One day about this time as another great crowd gathered, the people ran out of food again. Jesus called his disciples to discuss the situation. "I pity these people," he said, "for they have been here three days, and have nothing

left to eat. [3]And if I send them home without feeding them, they will faint along the road! For some of them have come a long distance."

[4]"Are we supposed to find food for them here in the desert?" his disciples scoffed.

[5]"How many loaves of bread do you have?" he asked.

"Seven," they replied. [6]So he told the crowd to sit down on the ground. Then he took the seven loaves, thanked God for them, broke them into pieces and passed them to his disciples; and the disciples placed them before the people. [7]A few small fish were found, too, so Jesus also blessed these and told the disciples to serve them.

MATT. 15

[37,38]And everyone ate until full — 4,000 men besides the women and children! And afterwards, when the scraps were picked up, there were seven basketfuls left over!

[39]Then Jesus sent the people home and got into the boat and crossed to Magdalan.

MATT. 16

The Jewish Leaders Demand a Sign

[1]One day the Pharisees and Sadducees came to test Jesus' claim of being the Messiah by asking him to show them some great demonstrations in the skies.

[2,3]He replied, "You are good at reading the weather signs of the skies — red sky tonight means fair weather tomorrow; red sky in the morning means foul weather all day — but you can't read the obvious signs of the times! [4]This evil, unbelieving nation is asking for some strange sign in the heavens, but no further proof will be given except the miracle that happened to Jonah." Then Jesus walked out on them.

The Yeast of the Pharisees and Sadducees

[5]Arriving across the lake, the disciples discovered they had forgotten to bring any food.

[6]"Watch out!" Jesus warned them; "beware of the yeast of the Pharisees and Sadducees."

[7]They thought he was saying this because they had forgotten to bring bread.

[8]Jesus knew what they were thinking and told them, "O men of little faith! Why are you so worried about having no food? [9]Won't you ever understand? Don't you remember at all the 5,000 I fed with the five loaves, and the basketfuls left over? [10]Don't you remember the 4,000 I fed, and all that was left? [11]How could you even think I was talking about food? But again I say, 'Beware of the yeast of the Pharisees and the Sadducees.' "

[12]Then at last they understood that by "yeast" he meant the *wrong teaching* of the Pharisees and Sadducees.

MARK 8

Jesus Heals a Blind Man at Bethsaida

[22]When they arrived at Bethsaida, some people brought a blind man to him and begged him to touch and heal him. [23]Jesus took the blind man by the hand and led him out of the village, and spat upon his eyes, and laid his hands over them.

"Can you see anything now?" Jesus asked him.

[24]The man looked around. "Yes!" he said, I see men! But I can't see them very clearly; they look like tree trunks walking around!"

[25]Then Jesus placed his hands over the man's eyes again and as the man stared intently, his sight was completely restored, and he saw everything clearly, drinking in the sights around him.

²⁶Jesus sent him home to his family. "Don't even go back to the village first," he said.

MATT. 16

A Revelation to Peter

¹³When Jesus came to Caesarea Philippi, he asked his disciples, "Who are the people saying I am?"

¹⁴"Well," they replied, "some say John the Baptist; some Elijah; some, Jeremiah or one of the other prophets."

¹⁵Then he asked them, "Who do *you* think I am?"

¹⁶Simon Peter answered, "The Christ, the Messiah, the Son of the living God."

¹⁷"God has blessed you, Simon, son of Jonah, " Jesus said, "for my Father in heaven has personally revealed this to you — this is not from any human source. ¹⁸You are Peter, a stone; and upon this rock I will build my church; and all the powers of hell shall not prevail against it. ¹⁹And I will give you the keys of the Kingdom of Heaven; whatever doors you lock on earth shall be locked in heaven; and whatever doors you open on earth shall be open in heaven!"

²⁰Then he warned his disciples against telling others that he was the Messiah.

MARK 8

Jesus Speaks of His Death

³¹Then he began to tell them about the terrible things he would suffer, and that he would be rejected by the elders and the Chief Priests and the other Jewish leaders — and be killed, and that he would rise again three days afterwards. ³²He talked about it quite frankly with them, so Peter took him aside and chided him. "You shouldn't say things like that," he told Jesus.

³³Jesus turned and looked at his disciples and then said to Peter very sternly, "Satan, get behind me! You are look-

ing at this only from a human point of view and not from God's."

³⁴Then he called his disciples and the crowds to come over and listen. "If any of you wants to be my follower," he told them, "you must put aside your own pleasures and shoulder your cross, and follow me closely. ³⁵If you insist on saving your life, you will lose it. Only those who throw away their lives for my sake and for the sake of the Good News will ever know what it means to really live.

³⁶"And how does a man benefit if he gains the whole world and loses his soul in the process? ³⁷For is anything worth more than his soul? ³⁸And anyone who is ashamed of me and my message in these days of unbelief and sin, I, the Messiah, will be ashamed of him when I return in the glory of my Father, with the holy angels."

MARK 9

¹Jesus went on to say to his disciples, "Some of you who are standing here right now will live to see the Kingdom of God arrive in great power!"

LUKE 9

The Transfiguration of Jesus

²⁸Eight days later he took Peter, James, and John with him into the hills to pray. ²⁹And as he was praying, his face began to shine, and his clothes became dazzling white and blazed with light. ³⁰Then two men appeared and began talking with him — Moses and Elijah! ³¹They were splendid in appearance, glorious to see; and they were speaking of his death at Jerusalem, to be carried out in accordance with God's plan.

³²Peter and the others had been very drowsy and had fallen asleep. Now they woke up and saw Jesus covered with brightness and glory, and the two men standing with him.

[33]As Moses and Elijah were starting to leave, Peter, all con-fused and not even knowing what he was saying, blurted out, "Master, this is wonderful! We'll put up three shelters — one for you and one for Moses and one for Elijah!"

[34]But even as he was saying this, a bright cloud formed above them; and terror gripped them as it covered them. [35]And a voice from the cloud said, "*This* is my Son, my Chosen One; listen to *him*."

[36]Then, as the voice died away, Jesus was there alone with his disciples...

MARK 9

[9]As they descended the mountainside he told them never to mention what they had seen until after he had risen from the dead. [10]So they kept it to themselves, but often talked about it, and wondered what he meant by "rising from the dead."

[11]Now they began asking him about something the Jewish religious leaders often spoke of, that Elijah must return [before the Messiah could come]. [12,13]Jesus agreed that Elijah must come first and prepare the way — and that he had, in fact, already come! And that he had been terrib-ly mistreated, just as the prophets had predicted...

MATT 17

[13]Then the disciples realized he was speaking of John the Baptist.

MARK 9

A Demon-Possessed Child is Healed

[14]At the bottom of the mountain they found a great crowd surrounding the other nine disciples, as some Jewish leaders argued with them. [15]The crowd watched Jesus in

awe as he came toward them, and then ran to greet him. ¹⁶"What's all the argument about?" he asked.

¹⁷One of the men in the crowd spoke up and said, "Teacher, I brought my son for you to heal — he can't talk because he is possessed by a demon. ¹⁸And whenever the demon is in control of him it dashes him to the ground and makes him foam at the mouth and grind his teeth and become rigid. So I begged your disciples to cast out the demon, but they couldn't do it."

¹⁹Jesus said [to his disciples], "Oh, what tiny faith you have; how much longer must I be with you until you believe? How much longer must I be patient with you? Bring the boy to me."

²⁰So they brought the boy, but when he saw Jesus the demon convulsed the child horribly, and he fell to the ground writhing and foaming at the mouth.

²¹"How long has he been this way?" Jesus asked the father.

And he replied, "Since he has been very small, ²²and the demon often makes him fall into the fire or into water to kill him. Oh, have mercy on us and do something if you can."

²³"If I can?" Jesus asked. *"Anything* is possible if you have faith."

²⁴The father instantly replied, "I *do* have faith; oh help me to have *more!"*

²⁵When Jesus saw the crowd was growing he rebuked the demon.

"O demon of deafness and dumbness," he said, "I command you to come out of this child and enter him no more!"

²⁶Then the demon screamed terribly and convulsed the boy again and left him; and the boy lay there limp and motionless, to all appearance dead. A murmur ran through the crowd — "He is dead." ²⁷But Jesus took him by the hand and

helped him to his feet and he stood up and was all right! [28]Afterwards, when Jesus was alone in the house with his disciples, they asked him, "Why couldn't we cast that demon out?"

[29]Jesus replied, "Cases like this require prayer."

LUKE 9

Jesus Speaks about His Death Again

[44]"Listen to me and remember what I say. I, the Messiah, am going to be betrayed." [45]But the disciples didn't know what he meant, for their minds had been sealed and they were afraid to ask him.

Chapter 14

MATT. 17

Peter Goes Fishing for Tax Money

24On their arrival in Capernaum, the Temple tax collectors came to Peter and asked him, "Doesn't your master pay taxes?"

25"Of course he does," Peter replied.

Then he went into the house to talk to Jesus about it, but before he had a chance to speak, Jesus asked him, "What do you think, Peter? Do kings levy assessments against their own people, or against conquered foreigners?"

26,27"Against the foreigners," Peter replied.

"Well, then," Jesus said, "the citizens are free! However, we don't want to offend them, so go down to the shore and throw in a line, and open the mouth of the first fish you catch. You will find a coin to cover the taxes for both of us; take it and pay them."

MARK 9

To Be the Greatest, Be the Least

33{In}... Capernaum... in the house where they were to stay he asked them, "What were you discussing out on the road?"

34But they were ashamed to answer, for they had been arguing about which of them was the greatest!

[35]He sat down and called them around him and said, "Anyone wanting to be the greatest must be the least — the servant of all!"

[36]Then he placed a little child among them; and taking the child in his arms he said to them...

LUKE 9

[48]..."Anyone who takes care of a little child like this is caring for me! And whoever cares for me is caring for God who sent me. Your care for others is the measure of your greatness."

MARK 9

"Anyone Who isn't Against Us is For Us"

[38]"One of his disciples, John, told him one day, "Teacher, we saw a man using your name to cast out demons; but we told him not to, for he isn't one of our group."

[39]"Don't forbid him!" Jesus said. "For no one doing miracles in my name will quickly turn against me. [40]Anyone who isn't against us is for us. [41]If anyone so much as gives you a cup of water because you are Christ's — I say this solemnly — he won't lose his reward.

Defend Against Temptation

[42]"But if someone causes one of these little ones who believe in me to lose faith — it would be better for that man if a huge millstone were tied around his neck and he were thrown into the sea.

[43,44]"If your hand does wrong, cut it off. Better live forever with one hand than be thrown into the unquenchable fires of hell with two! [45,46]If your foot carries you toward evil, cut it off! Better be lame and live forever than have two feet that carry you to hell.

[47]"And if your eye is sinful, gouge it out. Better enter the Kingdom of God half blind than have two eyes and see the fires of hell, [48]where the worm never dies, and the fire never goes out — [49]where all are salted with fire.

[50]"Good salt is worthless if it loses its saltiness; it can't season anything. So don't lose your flavor! Live in peace with each other."

LUKE 15

A Lost Sheep

[3,4]...Jesus used this illustration: "If you had a hundred sheep and one of them strayed away and was lost in the wilderness, wouldn't you leave the ninety-nine others to go and search for the lost one until you found it? [5]And then you would joyfully carry it home on your shoulders. [6]When you arrived you would call together your friends and neighbors to rejoice with you because your lost sheep was found.

[7]"Well, in the same way heaven will be happier over one lost sinner who returns to God than over ninety-nine others who haven't strayed away!

MATT. 18

When a Brother Sins

[15]"If a brother sins against you, go to him privately and confront him with his fault. If he listens and confesses it, you have won back a brother. [16]But if not, then take one or two others with you and go back to him again, proving everything you say by these witnesses. [17]If he still refuses to listen, then take your case to the church, and if the church's verdict favors you, but he won't accept it, then the church should excommunicate him. [18]And I tell you this — whatever you bind on earth is bound in heaven, and whatever you free on earth will be freed in heaven.

¹⁹"I also tell you this — if two of you agree down here on earth concerning anything you ask for, my Father in heaven will do it for you. ²⁰For where two or three gather together because they are mine, I will be right there among them."

The Unforgiving Debtor

²¹Then Peter came to him and asked, "Sir, how often should I forgive a brother who sins against me? Seven times?"

²²"No!" Jesus replied, "seventy times seven!

²³"The Kingdom of Heaven can be compared to a king who decided to bring his accounts up to date. ²⁴In the process, one of his debtors was brought in who owed him $10,000,000! ²⁵He couldn't pay, so the king ordered him sold for the debt, also his wife and children and everything he had.

²⁶"But the man fell down before the king, his face in the dust, and said, 'Oh, sir, be patient with me and I will pay it all.'

²⁷"Then the king was filled with pity for him and released him and forgave his debt.

²⁸"But when the man left the king, he went to a man who owed him $2,000 and grabbed him by the throat and demanded instant payment.

²⁹"The man fell down before him and begged him to give him a little time. 'Be patient and I will pay it,' he pled.

³⁰"But this creditor wouldn't wait. He had the man arrested and jailed him until the debt would be paid in full.

³¹"Then the man's friends went to the king and told him what had happened. ³²And the king called before him the man he had forgiven and said, 'You evil-hearted wretch! Here I forgave you all that tremendous debt, just because you asked me to — ³³shouldn't you have mercy on others, just as I had mercy on you?'

³⁴"Then the angry king sent the man to the torture chamber until he had paid every last penny due. ³⁵So shall my heavenly Father do to you if you refuse to truly forgive your brothers."

Chapter 15

JOHN 7

The Unbelief of Jesus' Brothers

¹After this, Jesus went to Galilee, going from village to village, for he wanted to stay out of Judea where the Jewish leaders were plotting his death. ²But soon it was time for the Tabernacle Ceremonies, one of the annual Jewish holidays, ³and Jesus' brothers urged him to go to Judea for the celebration.

"Go where people can see your miracles!" they scoffed. ⁴"You can't be famous when you hide like this! If you're so great, prove it to the world!" ⁵For even his brothers didn't believe in him.

⁶Jesus replied, "It is not the right time for me to go now. But you can go anytime and it will make no difference, ⁷for the world can't hate you; but it does hate me, because I accuse it of sin and evil. ⁸You go on, and I'll come later when it is the right time." ⁹So he remained in Galilee.

The Tabernacle Ceremonies

¹⁰But after his brothers had left for the celebration, then he went too, though secretly, staying out of the public eye. ¹¹The Jewish leaders tried to find him at the celebration and kept asking if anyone had seen him. ¹²There was a lot of discussion about him among the crowds. Some said, "He's a wonderful man," while others said, "No, he's duping

the public." [13]But no one had the courage to speak out for him in public for fear of reprisals from the Jewish leaders.

[14]Then, midway through the festival, Jesus went up to the Temple and preached openly. [15]The Jewish leaders were surprised when they heard him. "How can he know so much when he's never been to our schools?" they asked.

[16]So Jesus told them, "I'm not teaching you my own thoughts, but those of God who sent me. [17]If any of you really determines to do God's will, then you will certainly know whether my teaching is from God or is merely my own. [18]Anyone presenting his own ideas is looking for praise for himself, but anyone seeking to honor the one who sent him is a good and true person. [19]None of *you* obeys the laws of Moses! So why pick on *me* for breaking them? Why kill *me* for this?

[20]The crowd replied, "You're out of your mind! Who's trying to kill you?"

[21,22,23]Jesus replied, "I worked on the Sabbath by healing a man, and you were surprised. But you work on the Sabbath, too, whenever you obey Moses' law of circumcision (actually, however, this tradition of circumcision is older than the Mosaic law); for if the correct time for circumcising your children falls on the Sabbath, you go ahead and do it, as you should. So why should I be condemned for making a man completely well on the Sabbath? [24]Think this through and you will see that I am right."

Can This Be the Messiah?

[25]Some of the people who lived there in Jerusalem said among themselves, "Isn't this the man they are trying to kill?" [26]But here he is preaching in public, and they say nothing to him. Can it be that our leaders have learned, after all, that he really is the Messiah? [27]But how could he be? For we know where this man was born; when Christ

comes, he will just appear and no one will know where he comes from."

[28]So Jesus, in a sermon in the Temple, called out, "Yes, you know me and where I was born and raised, but I am the representative of one you don't know, and he is Truth. [29]I know him because I was with him, and he sent me to you."

[30]Then the Jewish leaders sought to arrest him; but no hand was laid on him, for God's time had not yet come.

[31]Many among the crowds at the Temple believed on him. "After all," they said, "what miracles do you expect the Messiah to do that this man hasn't done?"

Men Are Sent to Arrest Jesus

[32]When the Pharisees heard that the crowds were in this mood, they and the chief priests sent officers to arrest Jesus. [33]But Jesus told them, "[Not yet!] I am to be here a little longer. Then I shall return to the one who sent me. [34]You will search for me but not find me. And you won't be able to come where I am!"

[35]The Jewish leaders were puzzled by this statement. "Where is he planning to go?" they asked. "Maybe he is thinking of leaving the country and going as a missionary among the Jews in other lands, or maybe even to the Gentiles! [36]What does he mean about our looking for him and not being able to find him, and, 'You won't be able to come where I am'?"

Rivers of Living Water Shall Flow

[37]On the last day, the climax of the holidays, Jesus shouted to the crowds, "If anyone is thirsty, let him come to me and drink. [38]For the Scriptures declare that rivers of living water shall flow from the inmost being of anyone who believes in me." [39](He was speaking of the Holy Spirit, who would be given to everyone believing in him; but the Spirit

had not yet been given, because Jesus had not yet returned to his glory in heaven.)

The People are Divided about Jesus

⁴⁰When the crowds heard him say this, some of them declared, "This man surely is the prophet who will come just before the Messiah." ⁴¹,⁴²Others said, "He is the Messiah." Still others, "But he *can't* be! Will the Messiah come from *Galilee?* For the Scriptures clearly state that the Messiah will be born of the royal line of David, in *Bethlehem,* the village where David was born." ⁴³So the crowd was divided about him. ⁴⁴And some wanted him arrested, but no one touched him.

The Unbelief of the Jewish Leaders

⁴⁵The Temple police who had been sent to arrest him returned to the chief priests and Pharisees. "Why didn't you bring him in?" they demanded.

⁴⁶"He says such wonderful things!" they mumbled. "We've never heard anything like it."

⁴⁷"So you also have been led astray?" the Pharisees mocked. ⁴⁸"Is there a single one of us Jewish rulers or Pharisees who believes he is the Messiah? ⁴⁹These stupid crowds do, yes; but what do they know about it? A curse upon them anyway!"

⁵⁰Then Nicodemus spoke up. (Remember him? He was the Jewish leader who came secretly to interview Jesus.) ⁵¹"Is it legal to convict a man before he is even tried?" he asked.

⁵²They replied, "Are you a wretched Galilean too? Search the Scriptures and see for yourself—no prophets will come from Galilee!"

⁵³Then the meeting broke up and everybody went home.

JOHN 8

Jesus' Reaction to an Adulterous Woman

¹Jesus returned to the Mount of Olives, ²but early the next morning he was back again at the Temple. A crowd soon gathered, and he sat down and talked to them. ³As he was speaking, the Jewish leaders and Pharisees brought a woman caught in adultery and placed her out in front of the staring crowd.

⁴"Teacher," they said to Jesus, "this woman was caught in the very act of adultery. ⁵Moses' law says to kill her. What about it?"

⁶They were trying to trap him into saying something they could use against him, but Jesus stooped down and wrote in the dust with his finger. ⁷They kept demanding an answer, so he stood up again and said, "All right, hurl the stones at her until she dies. But only he who has never sinned may throw the first!"

⁸Then he stooped again and wrote some more in the dust. ⁹And the Jewish leaders slipped away one by one, beginning with the eldest, until only Jesus was left in front of the crowd with the woman.

¹⁰Then Jesus stood up again and said to her, "Where are your accusers? Didn't even one of them condemn you?"

¹¹"No, sir," she said.

And Jesus said, "Neither do I. Go and sin no more."

The Light of the World

¹²Later, in one of his talks, Jesus said to the people, "I am the Light of the world. So if you follow me, you won't be stumbling through the darkness, for living light will flood your path."

¹³The Pharisees replied, "You are boasting — and lying!"

[14]Jesus told them, "These claims are true even though I make them concerning myself. For I know where I came from and where I am going, but you don't know this about me. [15]You pass judgement on me without knowing the facts. I am not judging you now; [16]but if I were, it would be an absolutely correct judgement in every respect, for I have with me the Father who sent me. [17]Your laws say that if two men agree on something that has happened, their witness is accepted as fact. [18]Well, I am one witness, and my Father who sent me is the other."

[19]"Where is your father?" they asked.

Jesus answered, "You don't know who I am, so you don't know who my Father is. If you knew me, then you would know him too."

[20]Jesus made these statements while in the section of the Temple known as the Treasury. But he was not arrested, for his time had not yet run out.

"You Cannot Come Where I Am Going"

[21]Later he said to them again, "I am going away; and you will search for me, and die in your sins. And you cannot come where I am going."

[22]The Jews asked, "Is he planning suicide? What does he mean, 'You cannot come where I am going'?"

[23]Then he said to them, "You are from below; I am from above. You are of this world; I am not. [24]That is why I said that you will die in your sins; for unless you believe that I am the Messiah, the Son of God, you will die in your sins."

[25]"Tell us who you are," they demanded.

He replied, "I am the one I have always claimed to be. [26]I could condemn you for much and teach you much, but I won't, for I say only what I am told to by the one who sent me; and he is Truth." [27]But they still didn't understand that he was talking to them about God.

²⁸So Jesus said, "When you have killed the Messiah, then you will realize that I am he and that I have not been telling you my own ideas, but I have spoken what the Father taught me. ²⁹And he who sent me is with me — he has not deserted me — for I always do those things that are pleasing to him."

³⁰,³¹Then many of the Jewish leaders who heard him say these things began believing him to be the Messiah.

"The Truth Will Set You Free"

Jesus said to them, "You are truly my disciples if you live as I tell you to, ³²and you will know the truth, and the truth will set you free."

³³"But we are descendants of Abraham," they said, "and have never been slaves to any man on earth! What do you mean, 'set free'?"

³⁴Jesus replied, "You are the slaves of sin, every one of you. ³⁵And slaves don't have rights, but the Son has every right there is! ³⁶So if the Son sets you free, you will indeed be free — ³⁷(Yes, I realize that you are descendants of Abraham!) And yet some of you are trying to kill me because my message does not find a home within your hearts. ³⁸I am telling you what I saw when I was with my Father. But you are following the advice of *your* father."

Children of the Devil

³⁹"Our father is Abraham," they declared.

"No!" Jesus replied, "for if he were, you would follow his good example. ⁴⁰But instead you are trying to kill me — and all because I told you the truth I heard from God. Abraham wouldn't do a thing like that! ⁴¹No, you are obeying your *real* father when you act that way."

They replied, "We were not born out of wedlock — our true Father is God himself."

[42]Jesus told them, "If that were so, then you would love me, for I have come to you from God. I am not here on my own, but he sent me. [43]Why can't you understand what I am saying? It is because you are prevented from doing so! [44]For you are the children of your father the devil and you love to do the evil things he does. He was a murderer from the beginning and a hater of truth — there is not an iota of truth in him. When he lies, it is perfectly normal; for he is the father of liars. [45]And so when I tell the truth, you just naturally don't believe it!

[46]"Which of you can truthfully accuse me of one single sin? [No one!] And since I am telling you the truth, why don't you believe me? [47]Anyone whose Father is God listens gladly to the words of God. Since you don't, it proves you aren't his children."

"I Was In Existence Before Abraham was Ever Born"

[48]"You Samaritan! Foreigner! Devil!" the Jewish leaders snarled. "Didn't we say all along you were possessed by a demon?"

[49]"No," Jesus said, "I have no demon in me. For I honor my Father — and you dishonor me. [50]And though I have no wish to make myself great, God wants this for me and judges [those who reject me]. [51]With all the earnestness I have I tell you this — no one who obeys me shall ever die!"

[52]The leaders of the Jews said, "Now we know you are possessed by a demon. Even Abraham and the mightiest prophets died, and yet you say that obeying you will keep a man from dying! [53]So you are greater than our father Abraham, who died? And greater than the prophets, who died? Who do you think you are?" [54]Then Jesus told them this: "If I am merely boasting about myself, it doesn't count. But it is my Father — and you claim him as your God — who is saying these glorious things about me. [55]But you do not

even know him. I do. If I said otherwise, I would be as great a liar as you! But it is true — I know him and fully obey him. [56]Your father Abraham rejoiced to see my day. He knew I was coming and was glad."

[57]*The Jewish leaders:* "You aren't even fifty years old — sure, you've seen Abraham!"

[58]*Jesus:* "The absolute truth is that I was in existence before Abraham was ever born!"

[59]At that point the Jewish leaders picked up stones to kill him. But Jesus was hidden from them, and walked past them and left the Temple.

Chapter 16

James and John Are Rebuked

[51]As the time drew near for his return to heaven, he moved steadily onward toward Jerusalem with an iron will.

[52]One day he sent messengers ahead to reserve rooms for them in a Samaritan village. [53]But they were turned away! The people of the village refused to have anything to do with them because they were headed for Jerusalem.

[54]When word came back of what had happened, James and John said to Jesus, "Master, shall we order fire down from heaven to burn them up?" [55]But Jesus turned and rebuked them, [56]and they went on to another village.

The Cost of Discipleship

[57]As they were walking along, someone said to Jesus, "I will always follow you no matter where you go."

[58]But Jesus replied, "Remember, I don't even own a place to lay my head. Foxes have dens to live in, and birds have nests, but I, the Messiah, have no earthly home at all."

[59]Another time, when he invited a man to come with him and to be his disciple, the man agreed — but wanted to wait until his father's death.

[60]Jesus replied, "Let those without eternal life concern themselves with things like that. Your duty is to come and preach the coming of the Kingdom of God to all the world."

[61]Another said, "Yes, Lord, I will come, but first let me ask permission of those at home."

[62]But Jesus told him, "Anyone who lets himself be distracted from the work I plan for him is not fit for the Kingdom of God."

LUKE 10

Jesus Sends Out Seventy Disciples

[1]The Lord now chose seventy other disciples and sent them on ahead in pairs to all the towns and villages he planned to visit later.

[2]These were his instructions to them: "Plead with the Lord of the harvest to send out more laborers to help you, for the harvest is so plentiful and the workers so few. [3]Go now, and remember that I am sending you out as lambs among wolves. [4]Don't take any money with you, or a beggar's bag, or even an extra pair of shoes. And don't waste time along the way.

[5]"Whenever you enter a home, give it your blessing. [6]If it is worthy of the blessing, the blessing will stand; if not, the blessing will return to you.

[7]"When you enter a village, don't shift around from home to home, but stay in one place, eating and drinking without question whatever is set before you. And don't hesitate to accept hospitality, for the workman is worthy of his wages!

[8,9]"If a town welcomes you, follow these two rules:

(1) Eat whatever is set before you.

(2) Heal the sick; and as you heal them, say, 'The Kingdom of God is very near you now.'

[10]"But if a town refuses you, go out into its streets and say, [11]'We wipe the dust of your town from our feet as a public announcement of your doom. Never forget how close you were to the Kingdom of God!' [12]Even wicked

Sodom will be better off than such a city on the Judgement Day.

Judgement Against Unrepentant Cities Foretold

[13]"What horrors await you, you cities of Chorazin and Bethsaida! For if the miracles I did for you had been done in the cities of Tyre and Sidon, their people would have sat in deep repentance long ago, clothed in sackcloth and throwing ashes on their heads to show their remorse. [14]Yes, Tyre and Sidon will receive less punishment on the Judgement Day than you. [15]And you people of Capernaum, what shall I say about you? Will you be exalted to heaven? No, you shall be brought down to hell."

[16]Then he said to the disciples, "Those who welcome you are welcoming me. And those who reject you are rejecting me. And those who reject me are rejecting God who sent me."

The Seventy Return

[17]When the seventy disciples returned, they joyfully reported to him, "Even the demons obey us when we use your name."

[18]"Yes," he told them, "I saw Satan falling from heaven as a flash of lightning! [19]And I have given you authority over all the power of the Enemy, and to walk among serpents and scorpions and to crush them. Nothing shall injure you! [20]However, the important thing is not that demons obey you, but that your names are registered as the citizens of heaven."

Jesus is Filled with Joy

[21]Then he was filled with the joy of the Holy Spirit and said, "I praise you, O Father, Lord of heaven and earth, for hiding these things from the intellectuals and worldly wise and for revealing them to those who are as trusting as little

children. Yes, thank you, Father, for that is the way you wanted it. ²²I am the Agent of my Father in everything; and no one really knows the Son except the Father, and no one really knows the Father except the Son and those to whom the Son chooses to reveal him."

²³Then, turning to the twelve disciples, he said quietly, "How privileged you are to see what you have seen. ²⁴Many a prophet and king of old has longed for these days, to see and hear what you have seen and heard!"

The Story of the Good Samaritan

²⁵One day an expert on Moses' laws came to test Jesus' orthodoxy by asking him this question: "Teacher, what does a man need to do to live forever in heaven?"

²⁶Jesus replied, "What does Moses' law say about it?"

²⁷"It says," he replied, "that you must love the Lord your God with all your heart, and with all your soul, and with all your strength, and with all your mind. And you must love your neighbor just as much as you love yourself."

²⁸"Right!" Jesus told him. "*Do* this and *you* shall live!"

²⁹The man wanted to justify (his lack of love for some kinds of people), so he asked, "Which neighbors?"

³⁰Jesus replied with an illustration: "A Jew going on a trip from Jerusalem to Jericho was attacked by bandits. They stripped him of his clothes and money and beat him up and left him lying half dead beside the road.

³¹"By chance a Jewish priest came along; and when he saw the man lying there, he crossed to the other side of the road and passed him by. ³²A Jewish Temple-assistant walked over and looked at him lying there, but then went on.

³³"But a despised Samaritan came along, and when he saw him, he felt deep pity. ³⁴Kneeling beside him the Samaritan soothed his wounds with medicine and

bandaged them. Then he put the man on his donkey and walked along beside him till they came to an inn, where he nursed him through the night. [35]The next day he handed the inkeeper two twenty dollar bills and told him to take care of the man. 'If his bill runs higher than that,' he said, 'I'll pay the difference the next time I am here.'

[36]"Now which of these three would you say was a neighbor to the bandits' victim?"

[37]The man replied, "The one who showed him some pity."

Then Jesus said, "Yes, now go and do the same."

Visiting Martha and Mary

[38]As Jesus and the disciples continued on their way to Jerusalem they came to a village where a woman named Martha welcomed them into her home. [39]Her sister Mary sat on the floor, listening to Jesus as he talked.

[40]But Martha was the jittery type, and was worrying over the big dinner she was preparing.

She came to Jesus and said, "Sir, doesn't it seem unfair to you that my sister just sits here while I do all the work? Tell her to come and help me."

[41]But the Lord said to her, "Martha, dear friend, you are so upset over all these details! [42]There is really only one thing worth being concerned about. Mary has discovered it — and I won't take it from her!"

Chapter 17

JOHN 9

Jesus Heals a Blind Man

[1]As he was walking along, he saw a man blind from birth. [2]"Master," his disciples asked him, "why was this man born blind? Was it a result of his own sins or those of his parents?"

[3]"Neither," Jesus answered. "But to demonstrate the power of God. [4]All of us must quickly carry out the tasks assigned us by the one who sent me, for there is little time left before the night falls and all work comes to an end. [5]But while I am still here in the world, I give it my light."

[6]Then he spat on the ground and made mud from the spittle and smoothed the mud over the blind man's eyes, [7]and told him, "Go and wash in the Pool of Siloam" (the word "Siloam" means "Sent"). So the man went where he was sent and washed and came back seeing!

[8]His neighbors and others who knew him as a blind beggar asked each other, "Is this the same fellow—that beggar?"

[9]Some said yes, and some said no. "It can't be the same man," they thought, "but he surely looks like him!"

And the beggar said, "I *am* the same man!"

[10]Then they asked him how in the world he could see. What had happened?

[11]And he told them, "A man they call Jesus made mud and smoothed it over my eyes and told me to go to the Pool of Siloam and wash off the mud. I did, and I can see!"

[12]"Where is he now?" they asked.

"I don't know," he replied.

The Pharisees Question the Man Who Was Healed

[13]Then they took the man to the Pharisees. [14]Now as it happened, this all occurred on a Sabbath. [15]Then the Pharisees asked him all about it. So he told them how Jesus had smoothed the mud over his eyes, and when it was washed away, he could see!

[16]Some of them said, "Then this fellow Jesus is not from God, because he is working on the Sabbath."

Others said, "But how could an ordinary sinner do such miracles?" So there was a deep division of opinion among them.

[17]Then the Pharisees turned on the man who had been blind and demanded, "This man who opened your eyes — who do you say he is?"

"I think he must be a prophet sent from God," the man replied.

[18]The Jewish leaders wouldn't believe he had been blind, until they called in his parents [19]and asked them, "Is this your son? Was he born blind? If so, how can he see?"

[20]His parents replied, "We know this is our son and that he was born blind, [21]but we don't know what happened to make him see, or who did it. He is old enough to speak for himself. Ask him."

[22,23]They said this in fear of the Jewish leaders who had announced that anyone saying Jesus was the Messiah would be excommunicated.

²⁴So for the second time they called in the man who had been blind and told him, "Give the glory to God, not to Jesus, for we know Jesus is an evil person."

²⁵I don't know whether he is good or bad," the man replied, "but I know this: *I was blind, and now I see!*"

²⁶"But what did he do?" they asked. "How did he heal you?"

²⁷"Look!" the man exclaimed. "I told you once; didn't you listen? Why do you want to hear it again? Do you want to become his disciples too?"

²⁸Then they cursed him and said, "You are his disciple, but we are disciples of Moses. ²⁹We know God has spoken to Moses, but as for this fellow, we don't know anything about him."

³⁰"Why, that's very strange!" the man replied. "He can heal blind men, and yet you don't know anything about him! ³¹Well, God doesn't listen to evil men, but he has open ears to those who worship him and do his will. ³²Since the world began there has never been anyone who could open the eyes of someone born blind. ³³If this man were not from God, he couldn't do it."

³⁴"You illegitimate bastard, you!" they shouted. "Are you trying to teach *us?*" And they threw him out.

Giving Sight to the Spiritually Blind

³⁵When Jesus heard what had happened, he found the man and said, "Do you believe in the Messiah?"

³⁶The man answered, "Who is he, sir, for I want to."

³⁷"You have seen him," Jesus said, "and he is speaking to you!"

³⁸"Yes, Lord," the man said, "I believe!" And he worshiped Jesus.

[39]Then Jesus told him, "I have come into the world to give sight to those who are spiritually blind and to show those who think they see that they are blind."

[40]The Pharisees who were standing there asked, "Are you saying we are blind?"

[41]"If you were blind, you wouldn't be guilty," Jesus replied. "But your guilt remains because you claim to know what you are doing.

JOHN 10

The Story of the Sheepfold

[1]"Anyone refusing to walk through the gate into a sheepfold, who sneaks over the wall, must surely be a thief! [2]For a shepherd comes through the gate. [3]The gatekeeper opens the gate for him, and the sheep hear his voice and come to him; and he calls his own sheep by name and leads them out. [4]He walks ahead of them; and they follow him, for they recognize his voice." [5]They won't follow a stranger but will run from him, for they don't recognize his voice."

[6]Those who heard Jesus use this illustration didn't understand what he meant, [7]so he explained it to them.

The Good Shepherd

"I am the Gate for the sheep," he said. [8]"All others who came before me were thieves and robbers. But the true sheep did not listen to them. [9]Yes, I am the Gate. Those who come in by way of the Gate will be saved and will go in and out and find green pastures. [10]The thief's purpose is to steal, kill and destroy. My purpose is to give life in all its fulness.

[11]"I am the Good Shepherd. The Good Shepherd lays down his life for the sheep. [12]A hired man will run when he sees a wolf coming and will leave the sheep, for they aren't his and he isn't their shepherd. And so the wolf leaps on

them and scatters the flock. [13]The hired man runs because he is hired and has no real concern for the sheep.

[14]"I am the Good Shepherd and know my own sheep, and they know me, [15]just as my Father knows me and I know the Father; and I lay down my life for the sheep. [16]I have other sheep, too, in another fold. I must bring them also, and they will heed my voice; and there will be one flock with one Shepherd.

[17]The Father loves me because I lay down my life that I may have it back again. [18]No one can kill me without my consent — I lay down my life voluntarily. For I have the right and power to lay it down when I want to and also the right and power to take it again. For the Father has given me this right."

[19]When he said these things, the Jewish leaders were again divided in their opinions about him. [20]Some of them said, "He has a demon or else is crazy. Why listen to a man like that?"

[21]Others said, "This doesn't sound like a man possessed by a demon! Can a demon open the eyes of blind men?"

The Jewish Leaders Reject Him Again

[22,23]It was winter, and Jesus was in Jerusalem at the time of the Dedication Celebration. He was at the Temple, walking through the section known as Solomon's Hall. [24]The Jewish leaders surrounded him and asked, "How long are you going to keep us in suspense? If you are the Messiah, tell us plainly."

[25]"I have already told you, and you don't believe me," Jesus replied. "The proof is in the miracles I do in the name of my Father. [26]But you don't believe me because you are not part of my flock. [27]My sheep recognize my voice, and I know them, and they follow me. [28]I give them eternal life and they shall never perish. No one shall snatch them away

from me, [29]for my Father has given them to me, and he is more powerful than anyone else, so no one can kidnap them from me. [30]I and the Father are one."

[31]Then again the Jewish leaders picked up stones to kill him.

[32]Jesus said, "At God's direction I have done many a miracle to help the people. For which one are you killing me?"

[33]They replied, "Not for any good work, but for blasphemy; you, a mere man, have declared yourself to be God."

[34,35,36]"In your own Law it says that men are gods!" he replied. "So if the Scripture, which cannot be untrue, speaks of those as gods to whom the message of God came, do you call it blasphemy when the one sanctified and sent into the world by the Father says, 'I am the Son of God'? [37]Don't believe me unless I do miracles of God. [38]But if I do, believe them even if you don't believe me. Then you will become convinced that the Father is in me, and I in the Father."

[39]Once again they started to arrest him. But he walked away and left them, [40]and went beyond the Jordan River to stay near the place where John was first baptizing. [41]And many followed him.

"John didn't do miracles," they remarked to one another, "but all his predictions concerning this man have come true." [42]And many came to the decision that he was the Messiah.

Chapter 18

LUKE 11

Jesus Teaches His Followers

¹Once when Jesus had been out praying, one of his disciples came to him as he finished and said, "Lord, teach us a prayer to recite just as John taught one to his disciples."

²And this is the prayer he taught them: "Father, may your name be honored for its holiness; send your Kingdom soon. ³Give us our food day by day. ⁴And forgive our sins — for we have forgiven those who sinned against us. And don't allow us to be tempted."

⁵,⁶Then, teaching them more about prayer, he used this illustration: "Suppose you went to a friend's house at midnight, wanting to borrow three loaves of bread. You would shout up to him, 'A friend of mine has just arrived for a visit and I've nothing to give him to eat.' ⁷He would call down from his bedroom, 'Please don't ask me to get up. The door is locked for the night and we are all in bed. I just can't help you this time.'

⁸"But I tell you this — though he won't do it as a friend, if you keep knocking long enough he will get up and give you everything you want — just because of your persistence. ⁹And so it is with prayer — keep on asking and you will keep on getting; keep on looking and you will keep on finding; knock and the door will be opened. ¹⁰Everyone who asks,

receives; all who seek, find; and the door is opened to everyone who knocks.

[11]"You men who are fathers — if your boy asks for bread, do you give him a stone? If he asks for fish, do you give him a snake? [12]If he asks for an egg, do you give him a scorpion? [Of course not!]

[13]"And if even sinful persons like yourselves give children what they need, don't you realize that your heavenly Father will do at least that much, and give the Holy Spirit to those who ask for him?"

A Divided Kingdom Cannot Stand

[14]Once, when Jesus cast out a demon from a man who couldn't speak, his voice returned to him. The crowd was enthusiastic, [15]but some said, "No wonder he can cast them out. He gets his power from Satan, the king of demons!" [16]Others asked for something to happen in the sky to prove his claim of being the Messiah.

[17]He knew the thoughts of each of them, so he said, "Any kingdom filled with civil war is doomed; so is a home filled with argument and strife. [18]Therefore, if what you say is true, that Satan is fighting against himself by empowering me to cast out his demons, how can his kingdom survive? [19]And if I am empowered by Satan, what about your own followers? For they cast out demons! Do you think this proves they are possessed by Satan? Ask *them* if you are right! [20]But if I am casting out demons because of power from God, it proves that the Kingdom of God has arrived.

[21]"For when Satan, strong and fully armed, guards his palace, it is safe — [22]until someone stronger and better-armed attacks and overcomes him and strips him of his weapons and carries off his belongings.

[23]"Anyone who is not for me is against me; if he isn't helping me, he is hurting my cause.

When an Unclean Spirit Returns

24"When a demon is cast out of a man, it goes to the deserts, searching there for rest; but finding none, it returns to the person it left, 25and finds that its former home is all swept and clean. 26Then it goes and gets seven other demons more evil than itself, and they all enter the man. And so the poor fellow is seven times worse off then he was before."

The Truly Blessed

27As he was speaking, a woman in the crowd called out, "God bless your mother — the womb from which you came, and the breasts that gave you suck!"

28He replied, "Yes, but even more blessed are all who hear the Word of God and put it into practice."

Evil People Seeking Proof

29,30As the crowd pressed in upon him, he preached them this sermon: "These are evil times, with evil people. They keep asking for some strange happening in the skies [to prove I am the Messiah], but the only proof I will give them is a miracle like that of Jonah, whose experiences proved to the people of Nineveh that God had sent him. My similar experience will prove that God has sent me to these people.

31"And at the Judgement Day the Queen of Sheba shall arise and point her finger at this generation, condemning it, for she went on a long, hard journey to listen to the wisdom of Solomon; but one far greater than Solomon is here [and few pay any attention].

32"The men of Nineveh, too, shall arise and condemn this nation, for they repented at the preaching of Jonah; and someone far greater than Jonah is here [but this nation won't listen].

Filled With Light Within

³³"No one lights a lamp and hides it! Instead, he puts it on a lampstand to give light to all who enter the room. ³⁴Your eyes light up your inward being. A pure eye lets sunshine into your soul. A lustful eye shuts out the light and plunges you into darkness. ³⁵So watch out that the sunshine isn't blotted out. ³⁶If you are filled with light within, with no dark corners, then your face will be radiant too, as though a floodlight is beamed upon you."

Jesus Accuses the Pharisees and Lawyers

³⁷,³⁸As he was speaking, one of the Pharisees asked him home for a meal. When Jesus arrived, he sat down to eat without first performing the ceremonial washing required by Jewish custom. This greatly surprised his host.

³⁹Then Jesus said to him, "You Pharisees wash the outside, but inside you are still dirty—full of greed and wickedness! ⁴⁰Fools! Didn't God make the inside as well as the outside? ⁴¹Purity is best demonstrated by generosity.

⁴²"But woe to you Pharisees! For though you are careful to tithe even the smallest part of your income, you completely forget about justice and the love of God. You should tithe, yes, but you should not leave these other things undone.

⁴³"Woe to you Pharisees! For how you love the seats of honor in the synagogues and the respectful greetings from everyone as you walk through the markets! ⁴⁴Yes, awesome judgement is awaiting you. For you are like hidden graves in a field. Men go by you with no knowledge of the corruption they are passing."

⁴⁵"Sir," said an expert in religious law who was standing there, "you have insulted my profession, too, in what you just said."

46"Yes," said Jesus, "the same horrors await you! For you crush men beneath impossible religious demands — demands that you yourselves would never think of trying to keep. 47Woe to you! For you are exactly like your ancestors who killed the prophets long ago. 48Murderers! You agree with your fathers that what they did was right — you would have done the same yourselves.

49"This is what God days about you: 'I will send prophets and apostles to you, and you will kill some of them and chase away the others.'

50"And you of this generation will be held resposible for the murder of God's servants from the founding of the world — 51from the murder of Abel to the murder of Zechariah who perished between the altar and the sanctuary. Yes, it will surely be charged against you.

52"Woe to you experts in religion! For you hide the truth from the people. You won't accept it for yourselves, and you prevent others from having a chance to believe it."

53,54The Pharisees and legal experts were furious; and from that time on they plied him fiercely with a host of questions, trying to trap him into saying something for which they could have him arrested.

LUKE 12

Don't Be Hypocrites

1Meanwhile the crowds grew until thousands upon thousands were milling about and crushing each other. He turned now to his disciples and warned them, "More than anything else, beware of these Pharisees and the way they pretend to be good when they aren't. But such hypocrisy cannot be hidden forever. 2It will become as evident as yeast in dough. 3Whatever they have said in the dark shall be heard in the light, and what you have whispered in the inner rooms shall be broadcast from the housetops for all to hear!

Fear God

[4]"Dear friends, don't be afraid of those who want to murder you. They can only kill the body; they have no power over your souls. [5]But I'll tell you whom to fear — fear God who has the power to kill and then cast into hell.

[6]"What is the price of five sparrows? A couple of pennies? Not much more than that. Yet God does not forget a single one of them. [7]And he knows the number of hairs on your head! Never fear, you are more valuable to him than a whole flock of sparrows.

Sharing the Faith

[8]"And I assure you of this: I, the Messiah, will publicly honor you in the presence of God's angels if you publicly acknowledge me here on earth as your Friend. [9]But I will deny before the angels those who deny me here among men. [10](Yet those who speak against me may be forgiven — while those who speak against the Holy Spirit shall never be forgiven.)

[11]"And when you are brought to trial before these Jewish rulers and authorities in the synagogues, don't be concerned about what to say in your defense, [12]for the Holy Spirit will give you the right words even as you are standing there."

The Story of the Rich Fool

[13]Then someone called from the crowd, "Sir, please tell my brother to divide my father's estate with me."

[14]But Jesus replied, "Man, who made me a judge over you to decide such things as that? Beware! Don't always be wishing for what you don't have. For real life and real living are not related to how rich we are."

16Then he gave this illustration: "A rich man had a fertile farm that produced fine crops. 17In fact, his barns were full to overflowing—he couldn't get everything in. He thought about his problem, 18and finally exclaimed, 'I know—I'll tear down my barns and build bigger ones! Then I'll have room enough. 19And I'll sit back and say to myself, "Friend, you have enough stored away for years to come. Now take it easy! Wine, women, and song for you!" '

20"But God said to him, 'Fool! Tonight you die. Then who will get it all?'

21"Yes, every man is a fool who gets rich on earth but not in heaven."

Don't Worry

22Then turning to his disciples he said, "Don't worry about whether you have enough food to eat or clothes to wear. 23For life consists of far more than food and clothes. 24Look at the ravens—they don't plant or harvest or have barns to store away their food, and yet they get along all right—for God feeds them. And you are far more valuable to him than any birds!

25"And besides, what's the use of worrying? What good does it do? Will it add a single day to your life? Of course not! 26And if worry can't even do such little things as that, what's the use of worrying over bigger things?

27"Look at the lilies! They don't toil and spin, and yet Solomon in all his glory was not robed as well as they are. 28And if God provides clothing for the flowers that are here today and gone tomorrow, don't you suppose that he will provide clothing for you, you doubters? 29And don't worry about food—what to eat and drink; don't worry at all that God will provide it for you. 30All mankind scratches for its daily bread, but your heavenly Father knows your needs.

³¹He will always give you all you need from day to day if you will make the Kingdom of God your primary concern.

Where Your Treasure Is, Your Heart Will Be

³²"So don't be afraid, little flock. For it gives your Father great happiness to give you the Kingdom. ³³Sell what you have and give to those in need. This will fatten your purses in heaven! And the purses of heaven have no rips or holes in them. Your treasures there will never disappear; no thief can steal them; no moth can destroy them. ³⁴Wherever your treasure is, there your heart and thoughts will also be.

Be Ready

³⁵"Be prepared — all dressed and ready — ³⁶for your Lord's return from the wedding feast. Then you will be ready to open the door and let him in the moment he arrives and knocks. ³⁷There will be great joy for those who are ready and waiting for his return. He himself will seat them and put on a waiter's uniform and serve them as they sit and eat! ³⁸He may come at nine o' clock at night — or even at midnight. But whenever he comes there will be joy for his servants who are ready!

³⁹"Everyone would be ready for him if they knew the exact hour of his return — just as they would be ready for a thief if they knew when he was coming. ⁴⁰So be ready all the time. For I, the Messiah, will come when least expected."

The Story of the Unfaithful Servant

⁴¹Peter asked, "Lord, are you talking just to us, or to everyone?"

⁴²,⁴³,⁴⁴And the Lord replied, "I'm talking to any faithful, sensible man whose master gives him the responsibility of feeding the other servants. If his master returns and finds that he has done a good job, there will be a reward — his master will put him in charge of all he owns.

[45]"But if the man begins to think, 'My Lord won't be back for a long time,' and begins to whip the men and women he is supposed to protect, and to spend his time at drinking parties and in drunkenness — [46]well, his master will return without notice and remove him from his position of trust and assign him to the place of the unfaithful. [47]He will be severely punished, for though he knew his duty he refused to do it.

[48]"But anyone who is not aware that he is doing wrong will be punished only lightly. Much is required from those to whom much is given, for their responsibility is greater.

Division Rather Than Peace

[49]"I have come to bring fire to the earth, and, oh, that my task were completed! [50]There is a terrible baptism ahead of me, and how I am pent up until it is accomplished!

[51]"Do you think I have come to give peace to the earth? *No!* Rather, strife and division! [52]From now on families will be split apart, three in favor of me, and two against — or perhaps the other way around. [53]A Father will decide one way about me; his son, the other; mother and daughter will disagree; and the decision of an honored mother-in-law will be spurned by her daughter-in-law."

Discerning God's Warnings

[54]Then he turned to the crowd and said, "When you see clouds beginning to form in the west, you say, 'Here comes a shower.' And you are right.

[55]"When the south wind blows you say, 'Today will be a scorcher,' And it is. [56]Hypocrites! You interpret the sky well enough, but you refuse to notice the warnings all around you about the crisis ahead. [57]Why do you refuse to see for yourselves what is right?

Agree With Your Accuser

[58]"If you meet your accuser on the way to court, try to settle the matter before it reaches the judge, lest he sentence you to jail; [59]for if that happens you won't be free again until the last penny is paid in full."

Chapter 19

LUKE 13

Leave Your Evil Ways or Perish

¹About this time he was informed that Pilate had butchered some Jews from Galilee as they were sacrificing at the Temple in Jerusalem.

²"Do you think they were worse sinners than other men from Galilee?" he asked. "Is that why they suffered? ³Not at all! And don't you realize that you also will perish unless you leave your evil ways and turn to God?

⁴"And what about the eighteen men who died when the Tower of Siloam fell on them? Were they the worst sinners in Jerusalem? ⁵Not at all! And you, too, will perish unless you repent."

The Story of the Barren Fig Tree

⁶Then he used this illustration: "A man planted a fig tree in his garden and came again and again to see if he could find any fruit on it, but he was always disappointed. ⁷Finally he told his gardener to cut it down. 'I've waited three years and there hasn't been a single fig!' he said. 'Why bother with it any longer? It's taking up space we can use for something else.'

⁸" 'Give it one more chance,' the gardener answered. 'Leave it another year, and I'll give it special attention and

plenty of fertilizer. [9]If we get figs next year, fine; if not, I'll cut it down.' "

Jesus Heals a Handicapped Woman on the Sabbath

[10]One Sabbath as he was teaching in a synagogue, [11]he saw a seriously handicapped woman who had been bent double for eighteen years and was unable to straighten herself.

[12]Calling her over to him Jesus said, "Woman, you are healed of your sickness!" [13]He touched her, and instantly she could stand straight. How she praised and thanked God!

[14]But the local Jewish leader in charge of the synagogue was very angry about it because Jesus had healed her on the Sabbath day. "There are six days of the week to work," he shouted to the crowd. "Those are the days to come for healing, not on the Sabbath!"

[15]But the Lord replied, "You hypocrite! You work on the Sabbath! Don't you untie your cattle from their stalls on the Sabbath and lead them out for water? [16]And is it wrong for me, just because it is the Sabbath day, to free this Jewish woman from the bondage in which Satan has held her for eighteen years?"

[17]This shamed his enemies. And all the people rejoiced at the wonderful things he did.

The Story of the Mustard Seed

[18]Now he began teaching them again about the Kingdom of God: "What is the Kingdom like?" he asked. "How can I illustrate it? [19]It is like a tiny mustard seed planted in a garden; soon it grows into a tall bush and the birds live among its branches.

The Story of the Yeast

[20,21]"It is like yeast kneaded into dough, which works unseen until it has risen high and light."

The Narrow Door

[22]He went from city to city and village to village, teaching as he went, always pressing onward toward Jerusalem.

[23]Someone asked him, "Will only a few be saved?"

And he replied, [24,25]"The door to heaven is narrow. Work hard to get in, for the truth is that many will try to enter but when the head of the house has locked the door, it will be too late. Then if you stand outside knocking, and pleading, 'Lord, open the door for us,' he will reply, 'I do not know you.'

[26]"'But we ate with you, and you taught in our streets,' you will say.

[27]"And he will reply, 'I tell you, I don't know you. You can't come in here, guilty as you are. Go away.'

[28]"And there will be great weeping and gnashing of teeth as you stand outside and see Abraham, Isaac, Jacob, and all the prophets within the Kingdom of God — [29]for people will come from all over the world to to take their places there. [30]And note this: some who are despised now will be greatly honored then; and some who are highly thought of now will be least important then."

Jesus Grieves over Jerusalem

[31]A few minutes later some Pharisees said to him, "Get out of here if you want to live, for King Herod is after you!"

[32]Jesus replied, "Go tell that fox that I will keep on casting out demons and doing miracles of healing today and tomorrow; and the third day I will reach my destination. [33]Yes, today, tomorrow, and the next day! For it wouldn't do for a prophet of God to be killed except in Jerusalem!

[34]"O Jerusalem, Jerusalem! The city that murders the prophets. The city that stones those sent to help her. How often I have wanted to gather your children together even as a hen protects her brood under her wings, but you wouldn't let me. [35]And now—now your house is left desolate. And you will never again see me until you say, 'Welcome to him who comes in the name of the Lord.'"

LUKE 14

Another Healing on the Sabbath

[1]One Sabbath as he was in the home of a member of the Jewish Council, the Pharisees were watching him like hawks to see if he would heal a man who was present who was suffering from dropsy.

[3]Jesus said to the Pharisees and legal experts standing around, "Well, is it within the Law to heal a man on the Sabbath day, or not?"

[4]And when they refused to answer, Jesus took the sick man by the hand and healed him and sent him away.

[5]Then he turned to them: "Which of you doesn't work on the Sabbath?" he asked. "If your cow falls into a pit, don't you proceed at once to get it out?"

[6]Again they had no answer.

"He Who Humbles Himself Shall be Honored"

[7]When he noticed that all who came to the dinner were trying to sit near the head of the table, he gave them this advice: [8]"If you are invited to a wedding feast, don't always head for the best seat. For if someone more respected than you shows up, [9]the host will bring him over to where you are sitting and say, 'Let this man sit here instead,' And you, embarrassed, will have to take whatever seat is left at the foot of the table!

[10]"Do this instead — start at the foot; and when your host sees you he will come and say, 'Friend, we have a better place than this for you!' Thus you will be honored in front of all the other guests. [11]For everyone who tries to honor himself shall be humbled; and he who humbles himself shall be honored." [12]Then he turned to his host. "When you put on a dinner," he said, "don't invite friends, brothers, relatives, and rich neighbors! For they will return the invitation. [13]Instead, invite the poor, the crippled, the lame, and the blind. [14]Then at the resurrection of the godly, God will reward you for inviting those who can't repay you."

The Story of the Great Feast

[15]Hearing this, a man sitting at the table with Jesus exclaimed, "What a privilege it would be to get into the Kingdom of God!"

[16]Jesus replied, "A man prepared a great feast and sent out many invitations. [17]When all was ready, he sent his servant around to notify the guests that it was time for them to arrive. [18]But they all began making excuses. One said he had just bought a field and wanted to inspect it, and asked to be excused. [19]Another said he had just bought five pair of oxen and wanted to try them out. [20]Another had just been married and for that reason couldn't come.

[21]"The servant returned and reported to his master what they had said. His master was angry and told him to go quickly into the streets and alleys of the city and to invite the beggars, crippled, lame, and blind. [22]But even then, there was still room.

[23]" 'Well, then,' said his master, 'go out into the country lanes and out behind the hedges and urge anyone you find to come, so that the house will be full. [24]For none of those I invited first will get even the smallest taste of what I had prepared for them.' "

How to Become a Disciple

[25]Great crowds were following him. He turned around and addressed them as follows: [26]"Anyone who wants to be my follower must love me far more than he does his own father, mother, wife, children, brothers, or sisters — yes, more than his own life — otherwise he cannot be my disciple. [27]And no one can be my disciple who does not carry his own cross and follow me.

[28]"But don't begin until you count the cost. For who would begin construction of a building without first getting estimates and then checking to see if he has enough money to pay the bills? [29]Otherwise he might complete only the foundation before running out of funds. And then how everyone would laugh!

[30]" 'See that fellow there?' they would mock. 'He started that building and ran out of money before it was finished!'

[31]"Or what king would ever dream of going to war without first sitting down with his counselors and discussing whether his army of 10,000 is strong enough to defeat the 20,000 men who are marching against him?

[32]"If the decision is negative, then while the enemy troops are still far away, he will send a truce team to discuss terms of peace. [33]So no one can become my disciple unless he first sits down and counts his blessings — and then renounces them all for me.

Flavorless Salt

[34]"What good is salt that has lost its saltiness? [35]Flavorless salt is fit for nothing — not even for fertilizer. It is worthless and must be thrown out. Listen well, if you would understand my meaning."

LUKE 15

The Story of the Lost Sheep

[1]Dishonest tax collectors and other notorious sinners often came to listen to Jesus' sermons; [2]but this caused complaints from the Jewish religious leaders and the experts on Jewish law because he was associating with such despicable people — even eating with them!

[3,4]So Jesus used this illustration...

MATT. 18

[12]"If a man has a hundred sheep, and one wanders away and is lost, what will he do? Won't he leave the ninety-nine others and go out into the hills to search for the lost one? [13]And if he finds it, he will rejoice over it more than over the ninety-nine others safe at home! [14]Just so, it is not my Father's will that even one of these little ones should perish.

LUKE 15

The Story of the Lost Coin

[8]"Or take another illustration: A woman has ten valuable silver coins and loses one. Won't she light a lamp and look in every corner of the house and sweep every nook and cranny until she finds it? [9]And then won't she call in her friends and neighbors to rejoice with her? [10]In the same way there is joy in the presence of the angels of God when one sinner repents."

The Story of the Prodigal Son

[11]To further illustrate the point, he told them this story: "A man had two sons. [12]When the younger told his father, 'I want my share of your estate now, instead of waiting until you die!' his father agreed to divide his wealth between his sons.

His Story

[13]"A few days later, this younger son packed all his belongings and took a trip to a distant land, and there wasted all his money on parties and prostitutes. [14]About the time his money was gone a great famine swept over the land, and he began to starve. [15]He persuaded a local farmer to hire him to feed his pigs. [16]The boy became so hungry that even the pods he was feeding the swine looked good to him. And no one gave him anything.

[17]"When he finally came to his senses, he said to himself, 'At home even the hired men have food enough and to spare, and here I am, dying of hunger! [18]I will go home to my father and say, "Father, I have sinned against both heaven and you, [19]and am no longer worthy of being called your son. Please take me on as a hired man." '

[20]"So he returned to his father. And while he was still a long distance away, his father saw him coming, and was filled with loving pity and ran and embraced him and kissed him.

[21]"His son said to him, 'Father, I have sinned against heaven and you, and am not worthy of being called your son —'

[22]"But his father said to the slaves, 'Quick! Bring the finest robe in the house and put it on him. And a jeweled ring for his finger; and shoes! [23]And kill the calf we have in the fattening pen. We must celebrate with a feast, [24]for this son of mine was dead and has returned to life. He was lost and is found.' So the party began.

[25]"Meanwhile, the older son was in the fields working; when he returned home, he heard dance music coming from the house, [26]and he asked one of the servants what was going on.

[27] " 'Your brother is back,' he was told, 'and your father has killed the calf we were fattening and has prepared a great feast to celebrate his coming home again unharmed.'

[28]"The older brother was angry and wouldn't go in. His father came out and begged him, [29]but he replied, 'All these years I've worked hard for you and never once refused to do a single thing you told me to; and in all that time you never gave me even one young goat for a feast with my friends. [30]Yet when this son of yours come back after spending your money on prostitutes, you celebrate by killing the finest calf we have on the place.'

[31] " 'Look, dear son,' his father said to him, 'you and I are very close, and everything I have is yours. [32]But it is right to celebrate. For he is your brother; and he was dead and has come back to life! He was lost and is found!' "

LUKE 16

The Story of the Dishonest Accountant

[1]Jesus now told this story to his disciples: "A rich man hired an accountant to handle his affairs, but soon a rumor went around that the accountant was thoroughly dishonest.

[2]"So his employer called him in and said, 'What's this I hear about your stealing from me? Get your report in order, for you are to be dismissed.'

[3]"The accountant thought to himself, 'Now what? I'm through here, and I haven't the strength to go out and dig ditches, and I'm too proud to beg. [4]I know just the thing! And then I'll have plenty of friends to take care of me when I leave!'

[5,6]"So he invited each one who owed money to his employer to come and discuss the situation. He asked the first one, 'How much do you owe him?' 'My debt is 850 gallons of olive oil,' the man replied. 'Yes, here is the contract

you signed,' the accountant told him. 'Tear it up and write another one for half that much!'

[7] " 'And how much do you owe him?' he asked the next man. 'A thousand bushels of wheat,' was the reply. 'Here,' the accountant said, 'take your note and replace it with one for only 800 bushels!'

[8] "The rich man had to admire the rascal for being so shrewd. And it is true that the citizens of this world are more clever [in dishonesty!] than the godly are. [9] But shall I tell *you* to act that way, to buy friendship through cheating? Will this ensure your entry into an everlasting home in heaven? [10] *No!* For unless you are honest in small matters, you won't be in large ones. If you cheat even a little, you won't be honest with greater responsibilities. [11] And if you are untrustworthy about worldly wealth, who will trust you with the true riches of heaven? [12] And if you are not faithful with other people's money, why should you be entrusted with money of your own?

[13] "For neither you nor anyone else can serve two masters. You will hate one and show loyalty to the other, or else the other way around — you will be enthusiastic about one and despise the other. You cannot serve both God and money."

[14] The Pharisees, who dearly loved their money, naturally scoffed at all this.

[15] Then he said to them, "You wear a noble, pious expression in public, but God knows your evil hearts. Your pretense brings you honor from the people, but it is an abomination in the sight of God.

The Law and the Kingdom

¹⁶"Until John the Baptist began to preach, the laws of Moses and the messages of the prophets were your guides. But John introduced the Good News that the Kingdom of God would come soon. And now eager multitudes are pressing in. ¹⁷But that doesn't mean that the Law has lost its force in even the smallest point. It is as strong and unshakable as heaven and earth.

Jesus Speaks about Divorce

¹⁸"So anyone who divorces his wife and marries someone else commits adultery, and anyone who marries a divorced woman commits adultery."

Lazarus and the Rich Man

¹⁹"There was a certain rich man, " Jesus said, "who was splendidly clothed and lived each day in mirth and luxury. ²⁰One day Lazarus, a diseased beggar, was laid at his door. ²¹As he lay there longing for scraps from the rich man's table, the dogs would come and lick his open sores. ²²Finally the beggar died and was carried by the angels to be with Abraham in the place of the righteous dead. The rich man also died and was buried, ²³and his soul went into hell. There, in torment, he saw Lazarus in the far distance with Abraham.

²⁴" 'Father Abraham,' he shouted, 'have some pity! Send Lazarus over here if only to dip the tip of his finger in water and cool my tongue, for I am in anguish in these flames.'

²⁵"But Abraham said to him, 'Son, remember that during your lifetime you had everything you wanted, and Lazarus had nothing. So now he is here being comforted and you are in anguish. ²⁶And besides, there is a great chasm separating us, and anyone wanting to come to you from here

is stopped at its edge; and no one over there can cross to us.'

²⁷"Then the rich man said, 'O Father Abraham, then please send him to my father's home — ²⁸for I have five brothers — to warn them about this place of torment lest they come here when they die.'

²⁹"But Abraham said, 'The Scriptures have warned them again and again. Your brothers can read them any time they want to.'

³⁰"The rich man replied, 'No, Father Abraham, they won't bother to read them. But if someone is sent to them from the dead, then they will turn from their sins.'

³¹"But Abraham said, 'If they won't listen to Moses and the prophets, they won't listen even though someone rises from the dead.' "

LUKE 17

Do Not Cause Others to Sin

¹"There will always be temptations to sin," Jesus said one day to his disciples, "but woe to the man who does the tempting. ²,³If he were thrown into the sea with a huge rock tied to his neck, he would be far better off than facing the punishment in store for those who harm these little children's souls. I am warning you!

"Rebuke your brother if he sins, and forgive him if he is sorry. ⁴Even if he wrongs you seven time a day and each time turns again and asks forgiveness, forgive him."

Faith the Size of a Mustard Seed

⁵One day the apostles said to the Lord, "We need more faith; tell us how to get it."

⁶"If your faith were only the size of a mustard seed," Jesus answered, "it would be large enough to uproot that

mulberry tree over there and send it hurtling into the sea! Your command would bring immediate results!

A Servant's Duty

7,8,9"When a servant comes in from plowing or taking care of sheep, he doesn't just sit down and eat, but first prepares his master's meal and serves him his supper before he eats his own. And he is not even thanked, for he is merely doing what he is supposed to do. [10]Just so, if you merely obey me, you should not consider yourselves worthy of praise. For you have simply done your duty!"

Chapter 20

Lazarus Dies and Is Raised Again

[1]Do you remember Mary, who poured the costly perfume on Jesus' feet and wiped them with her hair? Well, her brother Lazarus, who lived in Bethany with Mary and her sister Martha, was sick. [3]So the two sisters sent a message to Jesus telling him, "Sir, your good friend is very, very sick."

[4]But when Jesus heard about it he said, "The purpose of his illness is not death, but for the glory of God. I the Son of God, will receive glory from this situation."

[5]Although Jesus was very fond of Martha, Mary, and Lazarus, [6]he stayed where he was for the next two days and made no move to go to them. [7]Finally, after the two days, he said to his disciples, "Let's go to Judea."

[8]But his disciples objected. "Master," they said, only a few a days ago the Jewish leaders in Judea were trying to kill you. Are you going there again?"

[9]Jesus replied, "There are twelve hours of daylight every day, and during every hour of it a man can walk safely and not stumble. [10]Only at night is there danger of a wrong step, because of the dark." [11]Then he said, "Our friend Lazarus has gone to sleep, but now I will go and waken him!"

^{12,13}The disciples, thinking Jesus meant Lazarus was having a good night's rest, said, "That means he is getting better!" But Jesus meant Lazarus had died.

¹⁴Then he told them plainly, "Lazarus is dead. ¹⁵And for your sake, I am glad I wasn't there, for this will give you another opportunity to believe in me. Come, let's go to him."

¹⁶Thomas, nicknamed "The Twin," said to his fellow disciples, "Let's go too — and die with him."

I Am the One Who Gives Life

¹⁷When they arrived at Bethany, they were told that Lazarus had already been in his tomb for four days. ¹⁸Bethany was only a couple of miles down the road from Jerusalem, ¹⁹and many of the Jewish leaders had come to pay their respects and to console Martha and Mary on their loss. ²⁰When Martha got word that Jesus was coming, she went to meet him. But Mary stayed at home.

²¹Martha said to Jesus, "Sir, if you had been here, my brother wouldn't have died. ²²And even now it's not too late, for I know that God will bring my brother back to life again if you will only ask him to."

²³Jesus told her, "Your brother will come back to life again."

²⁴"Yes," Martha said, "when everyone else does, on Resurrection Day."

²⁵Jesus told her, "I am the one who raises the dead and gives them life again. Anyone who believes in me, even though he dies like anyone else, shall live again. ²⁶He is given eternal life for believing in me and shall never perish. Do you believe this, Martha?"

²⁷"Yes, Master," she told him. "I believe you are the Messiah, the Son of God, the one we have so long awaited."

Tears Come to Jesus' Eyes

[28]Then she left him and returned to Mary and, calling her aside from the mourners, told her, "He is here and wants to see you." [29]So Mary went to him at once.

[30]Now Jesus had stayed outside the village, at the place where Martha met him. [31]When the Jewish leaders who were at the house trying to console Mary saw her leave so hastily, they assumed she was going to Lazarus' tomb to weep; so they followed her.

[32]When Mary arrived where Jesus was, she fell down at his feet, saying, "Sir, if you had been here, my brother would still be alive."

[33]When Jesus saw her weeping and the Jewish leaders wailing with her, he was moved with indignation and deeply troubled. [34]"Where is he buried?" he asked them.

They told him, "Come and see." [35]Tears came to Jesus' eyes.

[36]"They were close friends," the Jewish leaders said. "See how much he loved him."

[37,38]But some said, "This fellow healed a blind man — why couldn't he keep Lazarus from dying?"

Lazarus Comes Back From the Dead

And again Jesus was moved with deep anger. Then they came to the tomb. It was a cave with a heavy stone rolled across its door.

[39]"Roll the stone aside," Jesus told them.

But Martha, the dead man's sister, said, "By now the smell will be terrible, for he has been dead four days."

[40]"But didn't I tell you that you will see a wonderful miracle from God if you believe?" Jesus asked her.

[41]So they rolled the stone aside. Then Jesus looked up to heaven and said, "Father, thank you for hearing me.

[42](You always hear me, of course, but I said it because of all these people standing here, so that they will believe you sent me.)" [43]Then he shouted, "Lazarus, come out!"

[44]And Lazarus came—bound up in the gravecloth, his face muffled in a head swath. Jesus told them, "Unwrap him and let him go!"

The Jewish Leaders Conspire Against Jesus

[45]And so at last many of the Jewish leaders who were with Mary and saw it happen, finally believed on him. [46]But some went away to the Pharisees and reported it to them.

[47]Then the chief priests and Pharisees convened a council to discuss the situation.

"What are we going to do?" they asked each other. "For this man certainly does miracles. [48]If we let him alone the whole nation will follow him—and then the Roman army will come and kill us and take over the Jewish government."

[49]And one of them, Caiaphas, who was the High Priest that year, said, "You stupid idiots—[50]let this one man die for the people—why should the whole nation perish?"

[51]This prophecy that Jesus should die for the entire nation came from Caiaphas in his position as High Priest—he didn't think of it by himself, but was inspired to say it. [52]It was a prediction that Jesus' death would not be for Israel only, but for all the children of God scattered around the world. [53]So from that time on the Jewish leaders began plotting Jesus' death.

[54]Jesus now stopped his public ministry and left Jerusalem; he went to the edge of the desert, to the village of Ephraim, and stayed there with his disciples.

Chapter 21

LUKE 17

Jesus Meets Ten Men with Leprosy

¹¹{A little later} ...they continued onward toward Jerusalem, {and} they reached the border between Galilee and Samaria, ¹²and as they entered a village there, ten lepers stood at a distance, ¹³crying out, "Jesus, sir, have mercy on us!"

¹⁴He looked at them and said, "Go to the Jewish priest and show him that you are healed!" And as they were going, their leprosy disappeared.

¹⁵One of them came back to Jesus, shouting, "Glory to God, I'm healed!" ¹⁶He fell flat on the ground in front of Jesus, face downward in the dust, thanking him for what he had done. This man was a despised Samaritan.

¹⁷Jesus asked, "Didn't I heal ten men? Where are the nine? ¹⁸Does only this foreigner return to give glory to God?"

¹⁹And Jesus said to the man, "Stand up and go; your faith has made you well."

The Kingdom of God Is Within You

²⁰One day the Pharisees asked Jesus, "When will the Kingdom of God begin?" Jesus replied, "The Kingdom of God isn't ushered in with visible signs. ²¹You won't be able

to say, 'It has begun here in this place or there in that part of the country.' For the Kingdom of God is within you."

[22]Later he talked again about this with his disciples. "The time is coming when you will long for me to be with you even for a single day, but I won't be here," he said. [23]"Reports will reach you that I have returned and that I am in this place or that; don't believe it or go out to look for me. [24]For when I return, you will know it beyond all doubt. It will be as evident as the lightning that flashes across the skies. [25]But first I must suffer terribly and be rejected by this whole nation.

[26]"[When I return] the world will be [as indifferent to the things of God] as the people were in Noah's day. [27]They ate and drank and married—everything just as usual right up to the day when Noah went into the ark and the flood came and destroyed them all

[28]"And the world will be as it was in the days of Lot: people went about their daily business—eating and drinking, buying and selling, farming and building—[29]until the morning Lot left Sodom. Then fire and brimstone rained down from heaven and destroyed them all. [30]Yes, it will be 'business as usual' right up to the hour of my return.

[31]"Those away from home that day must not return to pack; those in the fields must not return to town—[32]remember what happened to Lot's wife! [33]Whoever clings to his life shall lose it, and whoever loses his life shall save it. [34]That night two men will be asleep in the same room, and one will be taken away, the other left. [35,36]Two women will be working together at household tasks; one will be taken, the other left; and so it will be with men working side by side in the fields."

[37]"Lord, where will they be taken?" the disciples asked. Jesus replied, "Where the body is, the vultures gather!"

His Story

The Story of the Widow and the Judge

¹One day Jesus told his disciples a story to illustrate their need for constant prayer and to show them that they must keep praying until the answer comes.

²"There was a city judge," he said, "a very godless man who had great contempt for everyone. ³A widow of that city came to him frequently to appeal for justice against a man who had harmed her. ⁴,⁵The judge ignored her for a while, but eventually she got on his nerves.

" 'I fear neither God nor man,' he said to himself, 'but this woman bothers me. I'm going to see to it that she gets justice, for she is wearing me out with her constant coming!'"

⁶Then the Lord said, "If even an evil judge can be worn down like that, ⁷don't you think that God will surely give justice to his people who plead with him day and night? ⁸Yes! He will answer them quickly! But the question is: when I, the Messiah, return, how many will I find who have faith [and are praying]?"

The Story of the Pharisee and the Tax Collectors

⁹Then he told this story to some who boasted of their virtue and scorned everyone else:

¹⁰"Two men went to the Temple to pray. One was a proud, self-righteous Pharisee, and the other a cheating tax collector. ¹¹The proud Pharisee 'prayed' this prayer: 'Thank God, I am not a sinner like everyone else, especially like that tax collector over there! For I never cheat, I don't commit adultery, ¹²I go without food twice a week, and I give to God a tenth of everything I earn.'

¹³"But the corrupt tax collector stood at a distance and dared not even lift his eyes to heaven as he prayed, but beat

upon his chest in sorrow, exclaiming, 'God be merciful to me, a sinner.' [14]I tell you, this sinner, not the Pharisee, returned home forgiven! For the proud shall be humbled, but the humble shall be honored."

MATT. 19

Jesus Speaks about Divorce

[3]Some Pharisees came to interview him, and tried to trap him into saying something that would ruin him.

"Do you permit divorce?" they asked.

[4]"Don't you read the Scriptures?" he replied. "In them it is written that at the beginning God created man and woman, [5,6]and that a man should leave his father and mother, and be forever united to his wife. The two shall become one — no longer two, but one! And no man may divorce what God has joined together,"

[7]"Then, why," they asked, "did Moses say a man may divorce his wife by merely writing her a letter of dismissal?"

[8]Jesus replied, "Moses did that in recognition of your hard and evil hearts, but it was not what God had originally intended. [9]And I tell you this, that anyone who divorces his wife, except for fornication, and marries another, commits adultery."

[10]Jesus' disciples then said to him, "If that is how it is, it is better not to marry!"

[11]"Not everyone can accept this statement," Jesus said. "Only those whom God helps. [12]Some are born without the ability to marry, and some are disabled by men, and some refuse to marry for the sake of the Kingdom of Heaven. Let anyone who can, accept my statement."

His Story

"Let the Children Come to Me"

¹³Once when some mothers were bringing their children to Jesus to bless them, the disciples shooed them away, telling them not to bother him.

¹⁴But when Jesus saw what was happening he was very much displeased with his disciples and said to them, "Let the children come to me, for the Kingdom of God belongs to such as they. Don't send them away! ¹⁵I tell you as seriously as I know how that anyone who refuses to come to God as a little child will never be allowed into his Kingdom."

¹⁶Then he took the children into his arms and placed his hands on their heads and he blessed them.

Jesus Meets a Rich Man

¹⁷As he was starting on a trip, a man came running to him and knelt down and asked, "Good Teacher, what must I do to get to heaven?"

¹⁸"Why do you call me good?" Jesus asked. "Only God is truly good! ¹⁹But as for your question — you know the commandments: don't kill, don't commit adultery, don't steal, don't lie, don't cheat, respect your father and mother."

²⁰"Teacher," the man replied, "I've never once broken a single one of those laws."

²¹Jesus felt genuine love for this man as he looked at him. "You lack only one thing," he told him; "go and sell all you have and give the money to the poor — and you shall have treasure in heaven — and come, follow me."

²²Then the man's face fell, and he went sadly away, for he was very rich. ²³Jesus watched him go, then turned

around and said to his disciples, "It's almost impossible for the rich to get into the Kingdom of God!"

[24]This amazed them. So Jesus said it again: "Dear children, how hard it is for those who trust in riches to get into the Kingdom of God. [25]It is easier for a camel to go through the eye of a needle than for a rich man to enter the Kingdom of God."

[26]The disciples were incredulous! "Then who in the world can be saved, if not a rich man?" they asked.

[27]Jesus looked at them intently, then said, "Without God, it is utterly impossible. But with God everything is possible."

[28]Then Peter began to mention all that he and the other disciples had left behind. "We've given up everything to follow you," he said.

[29]And Jesus replied, "Let me assure you that no one has ever given up anything—home, brothers, sisters, mother, father, children, or property—for love of me and to tell others the Good News, [30]who won't be given back, a hundred times over, homes, brothers, sisters, mothers, children, and land—with persecutions!

"All these will be his here on earth, and in the world to come he shall have eternal life. [31]But many people who seem to be important now will be the least important then; and many who are considered least here shall be greatest there."

MATT. 20

Laborers in the Harvest Field

[1]Here is another illustration of the Kingdom of Heaven. "The owner of an estate went out early one morning to hire workers for his harvest field. [2]He agreed to pay them $20 a day and sent them out to work.

³"A couple of hours later he was passing a hiring hall and saw some men standing around waiting for jobs, ⁴so he sent them also into his fields, telling them he would pay them whatever was right at the end of the day. ⁵At noon and again around three o' clock in the afternoon he did the same thing.

⁶"At five o' clock that evening he was in town again and saw some more men standing around and asked them, 'Why haven't you been working today?'

⁷" 'Because no one hired us,' they replied.

" 'Then go on out and join the others in my fields,' he told them.

⁸"That evening he told the paymaster to call the men in and pay them, beginning with the last men first. ⁹When the men hired at five o' clock were paid, each received $20. ¹⁰So when the men hired earlier came to get theirs, they assumed they would receive much more. But they, too, were paid $20.

^{11,12}"They protested, 'These fellows worked only one hour, and yet you've paid them just as much as those of us who worked all day in the scorching heat.'

¹³" 'Friend,' he answered one of them, 'I did you no wrong! Didn't you agree to work all day for $20? ¹⁴Take it and go. It is my desire to pay all the same; ¹⁵is it against the law to give away my money if I want to? Should you be angry because I am kind?' ¹⁶And so it is that the last shall be first, and the first, last."

MARK 10

Jesus Speaks About His Death Once More

³²Now they were on the way to Jerusalem, and Jesus was walking along ahead; and as the disciples were following, they were filled with terror and dread.

Taking them aside, Jesus once more began describing all that was going to happen to him when they arrived at Jerusalem.

[33]"When we get there," he told them, "I, the Messiah, will be arrested and taken before the chief priests and the Jewish leaders, who will sentence me to die and hand me over to the Romans to be killed. [34]They will mock me and spit on me and flog me with their whips and kill me; but after three days I will come back to life again."

Chapter 22

James and John Ask a Favor

³⁵Then James and John, the sons of Zebedee, came over and spoke to him in a low voice. "Master," they said, "we want you to do us a favor."

³⁶"What is it?" he asked.

³⁷"We want to sit on the thrones next to yours in your kingdom," they said, "one at your right and the other at your left!"

³⁸But Jesus answered, "You don't know what you are asking! Are you able to drink from the bitter cup of sorrow I must drink from? Or to be baptized with the baptism of suffering I must be baptized with?"

³⁹"Oh, yes," they said, "we are!"

And Jesus said, "You shall indeed drink from my cup and be baptized with my baptism, ⁴⁰but I do not have the right to place you on thrones next to mine. Those appointments have already been made."

⁴¹When the other disciples discovered what James and John had asked, they were very indignant. ⁴²So Jesus called them to him and said, "As you know, the kings and great men of the earth lord it over the people; ⁴³but among you it is different. Whoever wants to be great among you must be your servant. ⁴⁴And whoever wants to be greatest of all must be the slave of all. ⁴⁵For even I, the Messiah, am not

here to be served, but to help others, and to give my life as a ransom for many."

Blind Bartimaeus is Healed

⁴⁶And so they reached Jericho. Later, as they left town, a great crowd was following. Now it happened that a blind beggar named Bartimaeus (the son of Timaeus) was sitting beside the road as Jesus was going by.

⁴⁷When Bartimaeus heard that Jesus from Nazareth was near, he began to shout out, "Jesus, Son of David, have mercy on me!"

⁴⁸"Shut up!" some of the people yelled at him.

But he only shouted the louder, again and again, "O Son of David, have mercy on me!"

⁴⁹When Jesus heard him he stopped there in the road and said, "Tell him to come here."

So they called the blind man. "You lucky fellow," they said, "come on, he's calling you!" ⁵⁰Bartimaeus yanked off his old coat and flung it aside, jumped up and came to Jesus.

⁵¹"What do you want me to do for you?" Jesus asked.

"O Teacher," the blind man said, "I want to see!"

⁵²And Jesus said to him, "All right, it's done. Your faith has healed you."

And instantly the blind man could see, and followed Jesus down the road!

LUKE 19

Jesus Meets Zacchaeus

¹{While at} ...Jericho, a man named Zacchaeus, one of the most influential Jews in the Roman tax-collecting business (and, of course, a very rich man), ³tried to get a look at Jesus, but he was too short to see over the crowds. ⁴So he ran ahead and climbed into a sycamore tree beside the road, to watch from there.

His Story

[5]When Jesus came by he looked up at Zacchaeus and called him by name! "Zacchaeus!" he said. "Quick! Come down! For I am going to be a guest in your home today!"

[6]Zacchaeus hurriedly climbed down and took Jesus to his house in great excitement and joy.

[7]But the crowds were displeased. "He has gone to be the guest of a notorious sinner," they grumbled.

[8]Meanwhile, Zacchaeus stood before the Lord and said, "Sir, from now on I will give half my wealth to the poor, and if I find I have overcharged anyone on his taxes, I will penalize myself by giving him back four times as much!"

[9,10]Jesus told him, "This shows that salvation has come to this home today. This man was one of the lost sons of Abraham, and I, the Messiah, have come to search for and to save such souls as his."

The Story of the King's Money

[11]And because Jesus was nearing Jerusalem, he told a story to correct the impression that the Kingdom of God would begin right away.

[12]"A nobleman living in a certain province was called away to the distant capital of the empire to be crowned king of his province. [13]Before he left he called together ten assistants and gave them each $2000 to invest while he was gone. [14]But some of his people hated him and sent him their declaration of independence, stating that they had rebelled and would not acknowledge him as their king.

[15]"Upon his return he called in the men to whom he had given the money, to find out what they had done with it, and what their profits were.

[16]"The first man reported a tremendous gain—ten times as much as the original amount!

¹⁷" 'Fine!' the king exclaimed. 'You are a good man. You have been faithful with the little I entrusted to you, and as your reward, you shall be governor of ten cities.'

¹⁸"The next man also reported a splendid gain — five times the original amount.

¹⁹" 'All right!' his master said. 'You can be governor over five cities.'

²⁰"But the third man brought back only the money he had started with. 'I've kept it safe,' he said, ²¹"because I was afraid [you would demand my profits], for you are a hard man to deal with, taking what isn't yours and even confiscating the crops that others plant.' ²²'You vile and wicked slave,' the king roared. 'Hard, am I? That's exactly how I'll be toward you! If you knew so much about me and how tough I am, ²³then why didn't you deposit the money in the bank so that I could at least get some interest on it?'

²⁴"Then turning to the others standing by he ordered, 'Take the money away from him and give it to the man who earned the most!'

²⁵" 'But, sir, they said, 'he has enough already!'

²⁶" 'Yes,' the king replied, 'but it is always true that those who have, get more, and those who have little, soon lose even that. ²⁷And now about these enemies of mine who revolted — bring them in and execute them before me.' "

²⁸After telling this story, Jesus went on toward Jerusalem...

JOHN 11

⁵⁵The Passover, a Jewish Holy day, was near, and many country people arrived in Jerusalem several days early so that they could go through the cleansing ceremony before the Passover began. ⁵⁶They wanted to see Jesus, and as they gossiped in the Temple, they asked each other, "What do you think? Will he come for the Passover?" ⁵⁷Meanwhile

the chief priests and Pharisees had publicly announced that anyone seeing Jesus must report him immediately so that they could arrest him.

JOHN 12

Mary Anoints Jesus

[1]Six days before the Passover ceremonies began, Jesus arrived in Bethany where Lazarus was — the man he had brought back to life. [2]A banquet was prepared in Jesus' honor. Martha served, and Lazarus sat at the table with him. [3]Then Mary took a jar of costly perfume made from essence of nard, and anointed Jesus' feet with it and wiped them with her hair. And the house was filled with fragrance.

[4]But Judas Iscariot, one of his disciples — the one who would betray him — said, [5]"That perfume was worth a fortune. It should have been sold and the money given to the poor." [6]Not that he cared for the poor, but he was in charge of the disciples' funds and often dipped into them for his own use!

MARK 14

[6]But Jesus said, "Let her alone; why berate her for doing a good thing? [7]You always have the poor among you, and they badly need your help, and you can aid then whenever you want to; but I won't be here much longer.

[8]"She has done what she could, and has anointed my body ahead of time for burial. [9]And I tell you this in solemn truth, that wherever the Good News is preached throughout the world, this woman's deed will be remembered and praised."

JOHN 12

[9]When the ordinary people of Jerusalem heard of his arrival, they flocked to see him and also to see Lazarus — the

man who had come back to life again. [10]Then the chief priests decided to kill Lazarus too, [11]for it was because of him that many of the Jewish leaders had deserted and believed in Jesus as their Messiah.

Chapter 23

LUKE 19

The Triumphal Entry

²⁸...Jesus went on toward Jerusalem, walking along ahead of his disciples. ²⁹{And} ...he sent two disciples ahead, ³⁰with instructions to go to the next village, and as they entered, they were to look for a donkey tied beside the road. It would be a colt, not yet broken for riding.

"Untie him," Jesus said, "and bring him here. ³¹And if anyone asks you what you are doing, just say, 'The Lord needs him.' "

³²They found the colt as Jesus said, ³³and sure enough, as they were untying it, the owners demanded an explanation.

"What are you doing?" they asked. "Why are you untying our colt?"

³⁴And the disciples simply replied, "The Lord needs him!" ³⁵So they brought the colt to Jesus and threw some of their clothing across its back for Jesus to sit on.

^{36,37}Then the crowds spread out their robes along the road ahead of him, and as they reached the place where the road started down the Mount of Olives, the whole procession began to shout and sing as they walked along, praising God for all the wonderful miracles Jesus had done.

[38]"God has given us a King!" they exulted. "Long live the King! Let all heaven rejoice! Glory to God in the highest heavens!"

[39]But some of the Pharisees among the crowd said, "Sir, rebuke your followers for saying things like that!"

[40]He replied, "If they keep quiet, the stones along the road will burst into cheers!"

[41]But as they came closer to Jerusalem and he saw the city ahead, he began to cry. [42]"Eternal peace was within your reach and you turned it down," he wept, "and now it is too late. [43]Your enemies will pile up earth against your walls and encircle you and close in on you, [44]and crush you to the ground, and your children within you; your enemies will not leave one stone upon another – for you have rejected the opportunity God offered you."

MARK 11

[11]And so he entered into Jerusalem and went into the Temple. He looked around carefully at everything and then left – for it was now late in the afternoon – and went out to Bethany with the twelve disciples.

MARK 11

Jesus Curses a Fig Tree

[12]The next morning as they left Bethany, he felt hungry. [13]A little way off he noticed a fig tree in full leaf, so he went over to see if he could find any figs on it. But no, there were only leaves, for it was too early in the season for fruit.

[14]Then Jesus said to the tree, "You shall never bear fruit again!" And the disciples heard him say it.

Jesus Cleanses the Temple

[15]When they arrived back to Jerusalem he went to the Temple and began to drive out the merchants and their cus-

tomers {as he had done once before}, and knocked over the tables of the moneychangers and the stalls of those selling doves, [16]and stopped everyone from bringing in loads of merchandise.

[17]He told them, "It is written in the Scriptures, 'My Temple is to be a place of prayer for all nations,' but you have turned it into a den of robbers."

[18]When the chief priests and other Jewish leaders heard what he had done they began planning how best to get rid of him. Their problem was their fear of riots because the people were so enthusiastic about Jesus' teaching.

MATT. 21

[14]And now the blind and crippled came to him and he healed them there in the Temple. [15]But when the chief priests and other Jewish leaders saw these wonderful miracles, and heard even the little children in the Temple shouting, "God bless the Son of David," they were disturbed and indignant and asked him, "Do you hear what these children are saying?"

[16]"Yes," Jesus replied. "Didn't you ever read the Scriptures? For they say, 'Even little babies shall praise him!'"

[17]Then he returned to Bethany, where he stayed overnight.

Chapter 24

The Withered Fig Tree

[20]Next morning, as the disciples passed the fig tree he had cursed, they saw that it was withered from the roots! [21]Then Peter remembered what Jesus had said to the tree on the previous day, and exclaimed, "Look, Teacher! The fig tree you cursed has withered!"

[22,23]In reply Jesus said to his disciples, "If only you have faith in God — this is the absolute truth — you can say to this Mount of Olives, 'Rise up and fall into the Mediterranean,' and your command will be obeyed. All that's required is that you really believe and have no doubt! [24]Listen to me! You can pray for *anything,* and *if you believe, you have it;* it's yours! [25]But when you are praying, first forgive anyone you are holding a grudge against, so that your Father in heaven will forgive your sins too."

LUKE 20

The Jewish Leaders Question Jesus' Authority

[1]On one of those days when he was teaching and preaching the Good News in the Temple, he was confronted by the chief priests and other religious leaders and councilmen. [2]They demanded to know by what authority he had driven out the merchants from the Temple.

³"I'll ask you a question before I answer," he replied. ⁴"Was John sent by God, or was he merely acting under his own authority?"

⁵They talked it over among themselves. "If we say his message was from heaven, then we are trapped because he will ask, 'Then why didn't you believe him?' ⁶But if we say John was not sent from God, the people will mob us, for they are convinced that he was a prophet." ⁷Finally, they replied, "We don't know!"

⁸And Jesus responded, "Then I won't answer your question either."

MATT. 21

The Story of the Two Sons

²⁸"But what do you think about this? A man with two sons told the older boy, 'Son, go out and work on the farm today.' ²⁹'I won't,' he answered, but later he changed his mind and went. ³⁰Then the father told the youngest, 'You go!' and he said, 'Yes, sir, I will.' But he didn't. ³¹Which of the two was obeying his father?"

They replied, "The first, of course."

Then Jesus explained his meaning: "Surely evil men and prostitutes will get into the Kingdom before you do. ³²For John the Baptist told you to repent and turn to God, and you wouldn't, while very evil men and prostitutes did. And even when you saw this happening, you refused to repent, and so you couldn't believe.

The Story of the Wicked Farmers

³³"Now listen to this story: A certain landowner planted a vineyard with a hedge around it, and built a platform for the watchman, then leased the vineyard to some farmers on a sharecrop basis, and went away to live in another country.

³⁴"At the time of the grape harvest he sent his agents to the farmers to collect his share. ³⁵But the farmers attacked his men, beat one, killed one and stoned another.

³⁶"Then he sent a larger group of his men to collect for him, but the results were the same. ³⁷Finally the owner sent his son, thinking they would surely respect him.

³⁸"But when these farmers saw the son coming they said among themselves, 'Here comes the heir to this estate; come on, let's kill him and get it for ourselves!' ³⁹So they dragged him out of the vineyard and killed him.

⁴⁰"When the owner returns, what do you think he will do to those farmers?"

⁴¹The Jewish leaders replied, 'He will put the wicked men to a horrible death, and lease the vineyard to others who will pay him promptly."

The Honored Cornerstone

⁴²Then Jesus asked them, "Didn't you ever read in the Scriptures: 'The stone rejected by the builders has been made the honored cornerstone; how remarkable! what an amazing thing the Lord has done'?

⁴³"What I mean is that the Kingdom of God shall be taken away from you, and given to a nation that will give God his share of the crop. ⁴⁴All who stumble on this rock of truth shall be broken, but those it falls on will be scattered as dust."

⁴⁵When the chief priests and other Jewish leaders realized that Jesus was talking about them — that they were the farmers in his story — ⁴⁶they wanted to get rid of him, but were afraid to try because of the crowds, for they accepted Jesus as a prophet.

MATT. 22

The Story of the Wedding Banquet

¹Jesus told several other stories to show what the Kingdom of Heaven is like.

"For instance," he said, "it can be illustrated by the story of a king who prepared a great wedding dinner for his son. ³Many guests were invited, and when the banquet was ready he sent messengers to notify everyone that it was time to come. But all refused! ⁴So he sent other servants to tell them, 'Everything is ready and the roast is in the oven. Hurry!'

⁵"But the guests he had invited merely laughed and went on about their business, one to his farm, another to his store; ⁶others beat up his messengers and treated them shamefully, even killing some of them.

⁷"Then the angry king sent out his army and destroyed the murderers and burned their city. ⁸And he said to his servants, 'The wedding feast is ready, and the guests I invited aren't worthy of the honor. ⁹Now go out to the street corners and invite everyone you see.'

¹⁰"So the servants did, and brought in all they could find, good and bad alike; and the banquet hall was filled with guests. ¹¹But when the king came in to meet the guests he noticed a man who wasn't wearing the wedding robe [provided for him].

¹²" 'Friend,' he asked, 'how does it happen that you are here without a wedding robe?' And the man had no reply.

¹³"Then the king said to his aides, 'Bind him hand and foot and throw him out into the outer darkness where there is weeping and gnashing of teeth.' ¹⁴For many are called, but few are chosen.

Chapter Twenty-Four

Give Caesar What is Caesar's

[15]Then the Pharisees met together to try to think of some way to trap Jesus into saying something for which they could arrest him. [16]They decided to send some of their men along with the Herodians to ask him this question: "Sir, we know you are very honest and teach the truth regardless of the consequences, without fear or favor. [17]Now tell us, is it right to pay taxes to the Roman government or not?"

[18]But Jesus saw what they were after. "You hypocrites!" he exclaimed. "Who are you trying to fool with your trick questions? [19]Here, show me a coin." And they handed him a penny.

[20]"Whose picture is stamped on it?" he asked them. "And whose name is this beneath the picture?"

[21]"Caesar's," they replied.

"Well, then," he said, "give it to Caesar if it is his, and give God everything that belongs to God."

[22]His reply surprised and baffled them and they went away.

LUKE 20

The Sadducees Ask about the Resurrection

[27]Then some Sadducees — men who believed that death is the end of existence, that there is no resurrection — [28]came to Jesus with this:

"The laws of Moses state that if a man dies without children, the man's brother shall marry the widow and their children will legally belong to the dead man, to carry on his name. [29]We know of a family of seven brothers. The oldest married and then died without any children. [30]His brother married the widow and he, too, died. Still no children. [31]And so it went, one after the other, until each of the seven had married her and died, leaving no children. [32]Finally the woman died also. [33]Now here is our question: Whose wife will she be in the resurrection? For all of them were married to her!"

[34,35]Jesus replied, "Marriage is for people here on earth, but when those who are counted worthy of being raised from the dead get to heaven, they do not marry. [36]And they never die again; in these respects they are like angels, and are sons of God, for they are raised up in new life from the dead.

[37,38]"But as to your real question — whether or not there is a resurrection — why, even the writings of Moses himself prove this. For when he describes how God appeared to him in the burning bush, he speaks of God as 'the God of Abraham, the God of Isaac, and the God of Jacob.' To say that the Lord *is* some person's God means that person is *alive,* not dead! So from God's point of view, all men are living."

[39]"Well said, sir!" remarked some of the experts in the Jewish law who were standing there.

MARK 12

The Most Important Commandment

[28]One of the teachers of religion who was standing there listening to the discussion realized that Jesus had answered well. So he asked, "Of all the commandments, which is the most important?"

[29]Jesus replied, "The one that says, 'Hear, O Israel! The Lord our God is the one and only God. [30]And you must love him with all your heart and soul and mind and strength.'

[31]"The second is: 'You must love others as much as yourself.' No other commandments are greater than these."

[32]The teacher of religion replied, "Sir, you have spoken a true word in saying that there is only one God and no other. [33]And I know it is far more important to love him

with all my heart and understanding and strength, and to love others as myself, than to offer all kinds of sacrifices on the altar of the Temple."

[34]Realizing this man's understanding, Jesus said to him, "You are not far from the Kingdom of God."...

MATT. 22

Jesus Asks Them about David's Son

[41]Then, surrounded by the Pharisees, he asked them a question: [42]"What about the Messiah? Whose son is he?" "The son of David," they replied.

[43]"Then why does David, speaking under the inspiration of the Holy Spirit, call him 'Lord'?" Jesus asked. For David said,

[44]"God said to my Lord, Sit at my right hand until I put your enemies beneath your feet.'

[45]Since David called him 'Lord,' how can he be merely his son?

[46]They had no answer. And after that no one dared ask him any more questions.

Chapter 25

Jesus Condemns the Religious Leaders

[1]Then Jesus said to the crowds, and to his disciples, [2]"You would think these Jewish leaders and these Pharisees were Moses, the way they keep making up so many laws! [3]And of course you should obey their every whim! It may be all right to do what they say, but above any-thing else, *don't follow their example.* For they don't do what they tell you to do. [4]They load you with impossible demands that they themselves don't even try to keep.

[5]"Everything they do is done for show. They act holy by wearing on their arms little prayer boxes with Scripture ver-ses inside, and by lengthening the memorial fringes of their robes. [6]And how they love to sit at the head table at ban-quets, and in the reserved pews in the synagogue! [7]How they enjoy the deference paid them on the streets, and to be called 'Rabbi' and 'Master'! [8]Don't let anyone ever call you that. For only God is your Rabbi and all of you are on the same level, as brothers. [9]And don't address anyone here on earth as 'Father,' for only God in heaven should be ad-dressed like that. [10]And don't be called 'Master,' for only one is your master, even the Messiah.

[11]"The more lowly your service to others, the greater you are. To be the greatest, be a servant. [12]But those who think

themselves great shall be disappointed and humbled; and those who humble themselves shall be exalted.

[13,14]"Woe to you, Pharisees, and you other religious leaders. Hypocrites! For you won't let others enter the Kingdom of Heaven, and you won't go in yourselves. And you pretend to be holy, with all your long, public prayers in the streets, while you are evicting widows from their homes. Hypocrites! [15]Yes, woe upon you hypocrites. For you go to all lengths to make one convert, and then turn him into twice the son of hell you are yourselves. [16]Blind guides! Woe upon you! For your rule is that to swear 'By God's Temple' means nothing—you can break that oath, but to swear 'By the gold in the Temple' is binding! [17]Blind fools! Which is greater, the gold, or the Temple that sanctifies the gold? [18]And you say that to take an oath 'By the altar' can be broken, but to swear 'By the gifts on the altar' is binding! [19]Blind! For which is greater, the gift on the altar, or the altar itself that sanctifies the gift? [20]When you swear 'By the altar' you are swearing by it and everything on it, [21]and when you swear 'By the Temple' you are swearing by it, and by God who lives in it. [22]And when you swear 'By heavens' you are swearing by the Throne of God and by God himself.

[23]"Yes, woe upon you, Pharisees, and you other religious leaders—hypocrites! For you tithe down to the last mint leaf in your garden, but ignore the important things—justice and mercy and faith. Yes, you should tithe, but you shouldn't leave the more important things undone. [24]Blind guides! You strain out a gnat and swallow a camel.

[25]"Woe to you, Pharisees, and you religious leaders—hypocrites! You are so careful to polish the outside of the cup, but the inside is foul with extortion and greed. [26]Blind

Pharisees! First cleanse the inside of the cup, and then the whole cup will be clean.

²⁷"Woe to you, Pharisees, and you religious leaders! You are like beautiful mausoleums — full of dead men's bones, and of foulness and corruption. ²⁸You try to look like saintly men, but underneath those pious robes of yours are hearts besmirched with every sort of hypocrisy and sin.

^{29,30}"Yes, woe to you, Pharisees, and you religious leaders — hypocrites! For you build monuments to the prophets killed by your fathers and lay flowers on the graves of the godly men they destroyed, and say, 'We certainly would never have acted as our fathers did.'

³¹"In saying that, you are accusing yourselves of being the sons of wicked men. ³²And you are following in their steps, filling up the full measure of their evil. ³³Snakes! Sons of vipers! How shall you escape the judgement of hell?

³⁴"I will send you prophets, and wise men, and inspired writers, and you will kill some by crucifixion, and rip open the backs of others with whips in your synagogues, and hound them from city to city, ³⁵so that you will become guilty of all the blood of murdered godly men from righteous Abel to Zechariah (son of Barachiah), slain by you in the Temple between the altar and the sanctuary. ³⁶Yes, all the accumulated judgement of the centuries shall break upon the heads of this very generation.

Jesus Grieves Over Jerusalem

³⁷"O Jerusalem, Jerusalem, the city that kills the prophets, and stones all those God sends to her! How often I have wanted to gather your children together as a hen gathers her chicks beneath her wings, but you wouldn't let me. ³⁸And now your house is left to you, desolate. ³⁹For I tell you this, you will never see me again until you are ready to welcome the one sent to you from God."

Chapter Twenty-Five

MARK 12

A Widow's Offering

[41]Then he went over to the collection boxes in the Temple and sat and watched as the crowds dropped in their money. Some who were rich put in large amounts. [42]Then a poor widow came and dropped in two pennies.

[43,44]He called his disciples to him and remarked, "That poor widow has given more than all those rich men put together! For they gave a little of their extra fat, while she gave up her last penny."

JOHN 12

Some Greeks Ask to Meet Jesus

[20]Some Greeks who had come to Jerusalem to attend the Passover [21]paid a visit to Philip, who was from Bethsaida, and said, Sir, we want to meet Jesus." [22]Philip told Andrew about it, and they went together to ask Jesus.

[23,24]Jesus replied that the time had not come for him to return to his glory in heaven, and that "I must fall and die like a kernel of wheat that falls into the furrows of the earth. Unless I die I will be alone — a single seed. But my death will produce many new wheat kernels — a plentiful harvest of new lives. [25]If you love your life down here — you will lose it. If you despise your life down here — you will exchange it for eternal glory.

[26]"If these Greeks want to be my disciples, tell them to come and follow me, for my servants must be where I am. And if they follow me, the Father will honor them.

Jesus Tells How He Will Die

[27]"Now my soul is deeply troubled. Shall I pray, 'Father, save me from what lies ahead'? But that is the very reason why I came! [28]Father, bring glory and honor to your name."

Then a voice spoke from heaven saying, "I have already done this, and I will do it again." [29]When the crowd heard the voice, some of them thought it was thunder, while others declared an angel had spoken to him.

[30]Then Jesus told them, "The voice was for your benefit, not mine. [31]The time of judgement for the world has come — and the time when Satan, the prince of this world, shall be cast out. [32]And when I am lifted up [on the cross], I will draw everyone to me." [33]He said this to indicate how he was going to die.

[34]"Die?" asked the crowd. "We understood that the Messiah would live forever and never die. Why are you saying he will die? What Messiah are you talking about?"

[35]Jesus replied, "My light will shine out for you just a little while longer. Walk in it while you can, and go where you want to go before the darkness falls, for then it will be too late for you to find your way. [36]Make use of the Light while there is still time; then you will become my light bearers."

The Jews Refuse Him

After saying these things, Jesus went away and was hidden from them.

[37]But despite all the miracles he had done, most of the people would not believe he was the Messiah. [38]This is exactly what Isaiah the prophet had predicted: "Lord, who will believe us? Who will accept God's mighty miracles as proof?" [39]But they couldn't believe, for as Isaiah also said: [40]"God has blinded their eyes and hardened their hearts so that they can neither see nor understand nor turn to me to heal them." [41]Isaiah was referring to Jesus when he made this prediction, for he had seen a vision of the Messiah's glory.

[42]However, even many of the Jewish leaders believed him to be the Messiah but wouldn't admit it to anyone be-

cause of their fear that the Pharisees would excommunicate them from the synagogue; [43]for they loved the praise of men more than the praise of God.

You Will Be Judged By What I Have Spoken

[44]Jesus shouted to the crowds, "If you trust me, you are really trusting God. [45]For when you see me, you are seeing the one who sent me. [46]I have come as a Light to shine in this dark world, so that all who put their trust in me will no longer wander in the darkness. [47]If anyone hears me and doesn't obey me, I am not his judge—for I have come to save the world and not to judge it. [48]But all who reject me and my message will be judged at the Day of Judgement by the truths I have spoken. [49]For these are not my own ideas, but I have told you what the Father said to tell you. [50]And I know his instructions lead to eternal life; so whatever he tells me to say, I say!"

Chapter 26

MATT. 24

A Sermon on the Mount of Olives

¹As Jesus was leaving the Temple grounds, his disciples came along and wanted to take him on a tour of the various Temple buildings

²But he told them, "All these buildings will be knocked down, with not one stone left on top of another!"

³"When will this happen?" the disciples asked him later, as he sat on the slopes of the Mount of Olives. "What events will signal your return, and the end of the world?"

⁴Jesus told them. "Don't let anyone fool you. ⁵For many will come claiming to be the Messiah, and will lead many astray. ⁶When you hear of wars beginning, this does not signal my return; these must come, but the end is not yet. ⁷The nations and kingdoms of the earth will rise against each other and there will be famines and earthquakes in many places. ⁸But all this will be only the beginning of the horrors to come.

⁹"Then you will be tortured and killed and hated all over the world because you are mine, ¹⁰and many of you shall fall back into sin and betray and hate each other. ¹¹And many false prophets will appear and lead many astray. ¹²Sin will be rampant everywhere and will cool the love of many. ¹³But those enduring to the end shall be saved.

[14]"And the Good News about the Kingdom will be preached throughout the whole world, so that all nations will hear it, and then, finally, the end will come.

[15]"So, when you see the horrible thing (told about by Daniel the prophet) standing in a holy place (Note to the reader: You know what is meant!), [16]then those in Judea must flee into the Judean hills. [17]Those on their porches must not even go inside to pack before they flee. [18]Those in the fields should not return to their homes for their clothes.

[19]"And woe to pregnant women and to those with babies in those days. [20]And pray that your flight will not be in winter, or on the Sabbath. [21]For there will be persecution such as the world has never before seen in all its history, and will never see again.

[22]"In fact, unless those days are shortened, all mankind will perish. But they will be shortened for the sake of God's chosen people.

[23]"Then if anyone tells you, 'The Messiah has arrived at such and such a place, or has appeared here or there,' don't believe it. [24]For false Christs shall arise, and false prophets, and will do wonderful miracles, so that if it were possible, even God's chosen ones would be deceived. [25]See, I have warned you.

[26]"So if someone tells you the Messiah has returned and is out in the desert, don't bother to go and look. Or, that he is hiding at a certain place, don't believe it! [27]For as the lightning flashes across the sky from east to west, so shall my coming be, when I, the Messiah, return. [28]And wherever the carcass is, there the vultures will gather.

The Signal of My Coming Will Appear

²⁹"Immediately after the persecution of those days the sun will be darkened, and the moon will not give light, and the stars will seem to fall from the heavens, and the powers overshadowing the earth will be convulsed.

³⁰"And then at last the signal of my coming will appear in the heavens and there will be deep mourning all around the earth. And the nations of the world will see me arrive in the clouds of heaven, with power and great glory. ³¹And I shall send forth my angels with the sound of a mighty trumpet blast, and they shall gather my chosen ones from the farthest ends of the earth and heaven.

³²"Now learn a lesson from the fig tree. When her branch is tender and the leaves begin to sprout, you know that summer is almost here. ³³Just so, when you see all these things beginning to happen, you can know that my return is near, even at the doors. ³⁴Then at last this age will come to its close.

³⁵"Heaven and earth will disappear, but my words remain forever.

Only the Father Knows

³⁶"But no one knows the date and hour when the end will be — not even the angels. No, not even God's Son. Only the Father knows.

^{37,38}"The world will be at ease — banquets and parties and weddings — just as it was in Noah's time before the sudden coming of the flood; ³⁹people wouldn't believe what was going to happen until the flood actually arrived and took them all away. So shall my coming be.

⁴⁰"Two men will be working together in the fields, and one will be taken, the other left. ⁴¹Two women will be going

about their household tasks; one will be taken, the other left.

[42]"So be prepared, for you don't know what day your Lord is coming.

[43]"Just as a man can prevent trouble from thieves by keeping watch for them, [44]so you can avoid trouble by always being ready for my unannounced return.

The Evil Servant

[45]"Are you a wise and faithful servant of the Lord? Have I given you the task of managing my household, to feed my children day by day? [46]Blessings on you if I return and find you faithfully doing your work. [47]I will put such faithful ones in charge of everything I own!

[48]"But if you are evil and say to yourself, 'My Lord won't be coming for a while,' [49]and begin oppressing your fellow servants, partying and getting drunk, [50]your Lord will arrive unannounced and unexpected, [51]and severely whip you and send you off to the judgement of the hypocrites; there will be weeping and gnashing of teeth.

MATT. 25

The Story of the Ten Bridesmaids

[1]"The Kingdom of Heaven can be illustrated by the story of ten bridesmaids who took their lamps and went to meet the bridegroom. [2,3,4]But only five of them were wise enough to fill their lamps with oil, while the other five were foolish and forgot.

[5,6]"So, when the bridegroom was delayed, they lay down to rest until midnight, when they were roused by the shout, 'The bridegroom is coming! Come out and welcome him!'

[7,8]"All the girls jumped up and trimmed their lamps. Then the five who hadn't any oil begged the others to share with them, for their lamps were going out.

⁹"But the others replied, 'We haven't enough. Go instead to the shops and buy some for yourselves.'

¹⁰"But while they were gone, the bridegroom came, and those who were ready went in with him to the marriage feast, and the door was locked.

¹¹"Later, when the other five returned, they stood outside, calling, 'Sir, open the door for us!'

¹²"But he called back, 'Go away! It is too late!'

¹³"So stay awake and be prepared, for you do not know the date or moment of my return.

Faithfulness Is Rewarded

¹⁴"Again, the Kingdom of Heaven can be illustrated by the story of a man going into another country, who called together his servants and loaned them money to invest for him while he was gone.

¹⁵"He gave $5,000 to one, $2,000 to another, and $1,000 to the last — dividing it in proportion to their abilities — and then left on his trip. ¹⁶The man who received the $5,000 began immediately to buy and sell with it and soon earned another $5,000. ¹⁷The man with $2,000 went right to work, too, and earned another $2,000.

¹⁸"But the man who received the $1,000 dug a hole in the ground and hid the money for safekeeping.

¹⁹"After a long time their master returned from his trip and called them to him to account for his money. ²⁰The man to whom he had entrusted the $5,000 brought him $10,000.

²¹"His master praised him for good work. 'You have been faithful in handling this small amount,' he told him, 'so now I will give you many more responsibilities. Begin the joyous tasks I have assigned to you.'

²²"Next came the man who had received the $2,000, with the report, 'Sir, you gave me the $2,000 to use, and I have doubled it.'

²³" 'Good work,' his master said. 'You are a good and faithful servant. You have been faithful over this small amount, so now I will give you much more.'

^{24,25}"Then the man with the $1,000 came and said, 'Sir, I knew you were a hard man, and I was afraid you would rob me of what I earned, so I hid your money in the earth and here it is!'

²⁶"But his master replied, 'Wicked man! Lazy slave! Since you knew I would demand your profit, ²⁷you should at least have put my money into the bank so I could have some interest. ²⁸Take the money from this man and give it to the man with $10,000. ²⁹For the man who uses well what he is given shall be given more, and he shall have abundance. But from the man who is unfaithful, even what little responsibility he has shall be taken from him. ³⁰And throw the useless servant out into outer darkness: there shall be weeping and gnashing of teeth.'

Separating the Sheep from the Goats

³¹"But when I, the Messiah, shall come in my glory, and all the angels with me, then I shall sit upon my throne of glory. ³²And all the nations shall be gathered before me. And I will separate the people as a shepherd separates the sheep from the goats, ³³and place the sheep at my right hand, and the goats at my left.

³⁴"Then I, the King, shall say to those at my right, 'Come, blessed of my Father, into the Kingdom prepared for you from the founding of the world. ³⁵For I was hungry and you fed me; I was thirsty and you gave me water; I was a stranger and you invited me into your homes; ³⁶naked and you clothed me; sick and in prison, and you visited me.'

³⁷"Then these righteous ones will reply, 'Sir, when did we ever see you hungry and feed you? Or thirsty and give you anything to drink? ³⁸Or a stranger, and help you? Or

naked, and clothe you? [39]When did we ever see you sick or in prison, and visit you?'

[40]"And I, the King, will tell them, 'When you did it to these my brothers you were doing it to me! [41]Then I will turn to those on my left and say, 'Away with you, you cursed ones, into the eternal fire prepared for the devil and his demons. [42]For I was hungry and you wouldn't feed me; thirsty, and you wouldn't give me anything to drink; [43]a stranger, and you refused me hospitality; naked, and you wouldn't clothe me; sick, and in prison, and you didn't visit me.'

[44]"Then they will reply, 'Lord, when did we ever see you hungry or thirsty or a stranger or naked or sick or in prison, and not help you?'

[45]"And I will answer, 'When you refused to help the least of these my brothers, you were refusing to help me.'

[46]"And they shall go away into eternal punishment; but the righteous into everlasting life."

LUKE 21

[37,38]Every day Jesus went to the Temple to teach, and the crowds began gathering early in the morning to hear him. And each evening he returned to spend the night on the Mount of Olives.

MATT. 26

The Jewish Leaders Plot to Kill Jesus

[2]{Jesus said to his disciples,} "As you know, the Passover celebration begins in two days, and I shall be betrayed and crucified."

[3]At that very moment the chief priests and other Jewish officials were meeting at the residence of Caiaphas the High Priest, [4]to discuss ways of capturing Jesus quietly, and

killing him. [5]"But not during the Passover celebration," they agreed, "for there would be a riot."

MATT. 26

Judas Decides to Betray Jesus

[14]Then Judas Iscariot, one of the twelve apostles, went to the chief priests, [15]and asked, "How much will you pay me to get Jesus into your hands?" And they gave him thirty silver coins. [16]From that time on, Judas watched for an opportunity to betray Jesus to them.

Chapter 27

LUKE 22

The Last Supper

[7]Now the day of the Passover celebration arrived, when the Passover lamb was killed and eaten with the unleavened bread. [8]Jesus sent Peter and John ahead to find a place to eat their Passover meal.

[9]"Where do you want us to go?" they asked.

[10]And he replied, "As soon as you enter Jerusalem, you will see a man walking along carrying a pitcher of water. Follow him into the house he enters, [11]and say to the man who lives there, 'Our Teacher says for you to show us the guest room where he can eat the Passover meal with his disciples.' [12]He will take you upstairs to a large room all ready for us. That is the place. Go ahead and prepare the meal there."

[13]They went off to the city and found everything just as Jesus had said, and prepared the Passover supper.

[14]Then Jesus and the others arrived, and at the proper time all sat down together at the table; [15]and he said, "I have looked forward to this hour with deep longing, anxious to eat this Passover meal with you before my suffering begins. [16]For I tell you now that I won't eat it again until what it represents has occurred in the Kingdom of God."

JOHN 13

Jesus Washes the Disciples' Feet

[1]Jesus knew on the evening of Passover Day that it would be his last night on earth before returning to his Father. During supper the devil had already suggested to Judas Iscariot, Simon's son, that this was the night to carry out his plan to betray Jesus. Jesus knew that the Father had given him everything and that he had come from God and would return to God. And how he loved his disciples! [4]So he got up from the supper table, took off his robe, wrapped a towel around his loins, [5]poured water into a basin, and began to wash the disciples' feet and to wipe them with the towel he had around him.

[6]When he came to Simon Peter, Peter said to him, "Master, you shouldn't be washing our feet like this!"

[7]Jesus replied, "You don't understand now why I am doing it; some day you will."

[8]"No," Peter protested, "you shall never wash my feet!"

"But if I don't, you can't be my partner," Jesus replied.

[9]Simon Peter exclaimed, "Then wash my hands and head as well—not just my feet!"

[10]Jesus replied, "One who has bathed all over needs only to have his feet washed to be entirely clean. Now you are clean—but that isn't true of everyone here." [11]For Jesus knew who would betray him. That is what he meant when he said, "Not all of you are clean."

[12]After washing their feet he put on his robe again and sat down and asked, "Do you understand what I was doing? [13]You call me 'Master' and 'Lord,' and you do well to say it, for it is true. [14]And since I, the Lord and Teacher, have washed your feet, you ought to wash each other's feet. [15]I have given you an example to follow: do as I have done to you. How true it is that a servant is not greater than his

master. Nor is the messenger more important than the one who sends him. [17]You know these things — now do them! That is the path of blessing.

[18]"I am not saying these things to all of you; I know so well each one of you I chose. The Scripture declares, 'One who eats supper with me will betray me,' and this will soon come true. [19]I tell you this now so that when it happens, you will believe on me.

[20]"Truly, anyone welcoming my messenger is welcoming me. And to welcome me is to welcome the Father who sent me."

[21]Now Jesus was in great anguish of spirit and exclaimed, "Yes, it is true — one of you will betray me."

MATT. 26

[24]{Jesus continued,} "For I must die just as was prophesied, but woe to the man by whom I am betrayed. Far better for that one if he had never been born."

JOHN 13

[22]The disciples looked at each other, wondering whom he could mean. [23]Since I {John} was sitting next to Jesus at the table, being his closest friend, [24]Simon Peter motioned to me to ask him who it was who would do this terrible deed.

[25]So I turned and asked him, "Lord, who is it?"

[26]He told me, "It is the one I honor by giving the bread dipped in the sauce."

And when he had dipped it, he gave it to Judas, son of Simon Iscariot.

[27]As soon as Judas had eaten it, Satan entered into him. Then Jesus told him, "Hurry — do it now."

[28]None of the others at the table knew what Jesus meant. [29]Some thought that since Judas was their treasurer, Jesus was telling him to go and pay for the food or to give some

money to the poor. [30]Judas left at once, going out into the night.

LUKE 22

An Argument Over Who Would Be Greatest

[24]And they began to argue among themselves as to who would have the highest rank [in the coming Kingdom].

[25]Jesus told them, "In this world the kings and great men order their slaves around, and the slaves have no choice but to like it! [26]But among you, the one who serves you best will be your leader. [27]Out in the world the master sits at the table and is served by his servants. But not here! For I am your servant. [28]Nevertheless, because you have stood true to me in these terrible days, [29]and because my Father has granted me a Kingdom, I, here and now, grant you the right [30]to eat and drink at my table in that Kingdom; and you will sit on thrones judging the twelve tribes of Israel.

MARK 14

[22]As they were eating, Jesus took bread and asked God's blessing on it and broke it in pieces and gave it to them and said, "Eat it — this is my body."

[23]Then he took a cup of wine and gave thanks to God for it and gave it to them; and they all drank from it. [24]And he said to them, "This is my blood, poured out for many, sealing the new agreement between God and man. [25]I solemnly declare that I shall never again taste wine until the day I drink a different kind in the Kingdom of God."

[26]Then they sang a hymn and went out to the Mount of Olives.

JOHN 13

[31]...Jesus said, "My time has come; the glory of God will soon surround me — and God shall receive great praise be-

cause of all that happens to me. [32]And God shall give me his own glory, and this so very soon. [33]Dear, dear children, how brief are these moments before I must go away and leave you! Then, though you search for me, you cannot come to me — just as I told the Jewish leaders.

[34]"And so I am giving a new commandment to you now — love each other just as much as I love you. [35]Your strong love for each other will prove to the world that you are my disciples."

[36]Simon Peter said, "Master, where are you going?"

And Jesus replied, "You can't go with me now; but you will follow me later."

[37]"But why can't I come now?" he asked, "for I am ready to die for you."

LUKE 22

[31]"Simon, Simon, Satan has asked to have you, to sift you like wheat, [32]but I have pleaded in prayer for you that your faith should not completely fail. So when you have repented and turned to me again, strengthen and build up the faith of your brothers."

MARK 14

[27]"All of you will desert me," Jesus told them, "for God has declared through the Prophets, 'I will kill the Shepherd, and the sheep will scatter.' [28]But after I am raised to life again, I will go to Galilee and meet you there."

[29]Peter said to him, "I will never desert you no matter what the others do!"

[30]"Peter," Jesus said, "before the cock crows a second time tomorrow morning you will deny me three times."

[31]"No!" Peter exploded. "Not even if I have to die with you! I'll *never* deny you!" And all the others vowed the same.

Chapter Twenty-Seven

LUKE 22

Money, Clothes and a Sword

[35]Then Jesus asked them, "When I sent you out to preach the Good News and you were without money, duffle bag, or extra clothing, how did you get along?"

"Fine," they replied.

[36]"But now," he said, take a duffle bag if you have one, and your money. And if you don't have a sword, better sell your clothes and buy one! [37]For the time has come for this prophecy about me to come true: 'He will be condemned as a criminal!' Yes, everything written about me by the prophets will come true."

[38]"Master," they replied, "we have two swords among us."

"Enough!" he said.

Chapter 28

"I Am the Way"

[1]"Let not your heart be troubled. You are trusting God, now trust in me. [2,3]There are many homes up there where my Father lives, and I am going to prepare them for your coming. When everything is ready, then I will come and get you, so that you can always be with me where I am. If this weren't so, I would tell you plainly. [4]And you know where I am going and how to get there."

[5]"No, we don't," Thomas said. "We haven't any idea where you are going, so how can we know the way?"

[6]Jesus told him, "I am the Way — yes, and the Truth and the Life. No one can get to the Father except by means of me. [7]If you had known who I am, then you would have known who my Father is. From now on you know him — and have seen him!"

[8]Philip said, "Sir, show us the Father and we will be satisfied."

[9]Jesus replied, "Don't you even know who I am, Philip, even after all this time I have been with you? Anyone who has seen me has seen the Father! So why are you asking to see him? [10]Don't you believe that I am in the Father and the Father is in me? The words I say are not my own but are from my Father who lives in me. And he does his work through me. [11]Just believe it — that I am in the Father and

the Father is in me. Or else believe it because of the mighty miracles you have seen me do.

[12,13]"In solemn truth I tell you, anyone believing in me shall do the same miracles I have done, and even greater ones, because I am going to be with the Father. You can ask him for *anything*, using my name, and I will do it, for this will bring praise to the Father because of what I, the Son, will do for you. [14]Yes, ask *anything*, using my name, and I will do it!

The Holy Spirit Will Be the Comforter

[15,16]"If you love me, obey me; and I will ask the Father and he will give you another Comforter, and he will never leave you. [17]He is the Holy Spirit, the Spirit who leads into all truth. The world at large cannot receive him, for it isn't looking for him and doesn't recognize him. But you do, for he lives with you now and some day shall be in you. [18]No, I will not abandon you or leave you as orphans in the storm — I will come to you. [19]In just a little while I will be gone from the world, but I will still be present with you. For I will live again — and you will too. [20]When I come back to life again, you will know that I am in my Father, and you in me, and I in you. [21]The one who obeys me is the one who loves me; and because he loves me, my Father will love him; and I will too, and I will reveal myself to him."

[22]Judas (not Judas Iscariot, but his other disciple with that name) said to him, "Sir, why are you going to reveal yourself only to us disciples and not to the world at large?"

[23]Jesus replied, "Because I will only reveal myself to those who love me and obey me. The Father will love them too, and we will come to them and live with them. [24]Anyone who doesn't obey me doesn't love me. And remember, I am not making up this answer to your question! It is the answer given by the Father who sent me.

²⁵"I am telling you these things now while am still with you. ²⁶But when the Father sends the Comforter instead of me—and by the Comforter I mean the Holy Spirit—he will teach you much, as well as remind you of everything I myself have told you.

²⁷"I am leaving you with a gift—peace of mind and heart! And the peace I give isn't fragile like the peace the world gives. So don't be troubled or afraid. ²⁸Remember what I told you—I am going away, but I will come back to you again. If you really love me, you will be very happy for me, for now I can go to the Father, who is greater than I am. ²⁹I have told you these things before they happen so that when they do, you will believe [in me].

³⁰"I don't have much more time to talk to you, for the evil prince of this world approaches. He has no power over me, ³¹but I will freely do what the Father requires of me so that the world will know that I love the Father. Come, let's be going.

JOHN 15

The True Vine

¹"I am the true Vine, and my Father is the Gardener. ²He lops off every branch that doesn't produce. And he prunes those branches that bear fruit for even larger crops. ³He has already tended you by pruning you back for greater strength and usefulness by means of the commands I gave you. ⁴Take care to live in me, and let me live in you. For a branch can't produce fruit when severed from the vine. Nor can you be fruitful apart from me.

⁵"Yes, I am the Vine; you are the branches. Whoever lives in me and I in him shall produce a large crop of fruit. For apart from me you can't do a thing. ⁶If anyone separates from me, he is thrown away like a useless branch, withers, and is gathered into a pile with all the others and is burned.

⁷But if you stay in me and obey my commands, you may ask any request you like, and it will be granted! ⁸My true disciples produce bountiful harvests. This brings great glory to my Father.

⁹"I have loved you even as the Father has loved me. Live within my love. ¹⁰When you obey me you are living in my love, just as I obey my Father and live in his love. ¹¹I have told you this so that you will be filled with my joy. Yes, your cup of joy will overflow! ¹²I demand that you love each other as much as I love you. ¹³And here is how to measure it — the greatest love is shown when a person lays down his life for his friends; ¹⁴and you are my friends if you obey me. ¹⁵I no longer call you slaves, for a master doesn't confide in his slaves; now you are my friends, proved by the fact that I have told you everything the Father told me.

¹⁶"You didn't choose me! I chose you! I appointed you to go and produce lovely fruit always, so that no matter what you ask for from the Father, using my name, he will give it to you. ¹⁷I demand that you love each other, ¹⁸for you get enough hate from the world!

Hatred From the World

"But then, it hated me before it hated you. ¹⁹The world would love you if you belonged to it; but you don't — for I chose you to come out of the world, and so it hates you. ²⁰Do you remember what I told you? 'A slave isn't greater than his master!' So since they persecuted me, naturally they will persecute you. And if they had listened to me, they would listen to you! ²¹The people of the world will persecute you because you belong to me, for they don't know God who sent me.

²²"They would not be guilty if I had not come and spoken to them. But now they have no excuse for their sin. ²³Anyone hating me is also hating my Father. ²⁴If I hadn't

done such mighty miracles among them they would not be counted guilty. But as it is, they saw these miracles and yet hated both of us — me and my Father. [25]This has fulfilled what the prophets said concerning the Messiah, 'They hated me without reason.'

[26]"But I will send you the Comforter — the Holy Spirit, the source of all truth. He will come to you from the Father and will tell you all about me. [27]And you also must tell everyone about me, because you have been with me from the beginning.

JOHN 16

[1]"I have told you these things so that you won't be staggered [by all that lies ahead.] [2]For you will be excommunicated from the synagogues, and indeed the time is coming when those who kill you will think they are doing God a service. [3]This is because they have never known the Father or me. [4]Yes, I'm telling you these things now so that when they happen you will remember I warned you. I didn't tell you earlier because I was going to be with you for a while longer.

The Holy Spirit Shall Guide You

[5]"But now I am going away to the one who sent me; and none of you seems interested in the purpose of my going; none wonders why. [6]Instead you are only filled with sorrow. [7]But the fact of the matter is that it is best for you that I go away, for if I don't, the Comforter won't come. If I do, he will — for I will send him to you.

[8]"And when he has come he will convince the world of it's sin, and of the availability of God's goodness, and of deliverance from judgement. [9]The world's sin is unbelief in me; [10]There is righteousness available because I go to the Father and you shall see me no more; [11]there is deliverance

from judgement because the prince of this world has already been judged.

[12]"Oh, there is so much more I want to tell you, but you can't understand it now. [13]When the Holy Spirit, who is truth, comes, he shall guide you into all truth, for he will not be presenting his own ideas, but will be passing on to you what he has heard. He will tell you about the future. [14]He shall praise me and bring me great honor by showing you my glory. [15]All the Father's glory is mine; this is what I mean when I say that he will show you my glory.

Your Sorrow will Turn to Joy

[16]"In just a little while I will be gone, and you will see me no more; but just a little while after that, and you will see me again!"

[17,18]"Whatever is he saying?" some of his disciples asked. "What is this about 'going to the Father'? We don't know what he means."

[19]Jesus realized they wanted to ask him so he said, "Are you asking yourselves what I mean? [20]The world will greatly rejoice over what is going to happen to me, and you will weep. But your weeping shall suddenly be turned to wonderful joy [when you see me again]. [21]It will be the same joy as that of a woman in labor when her child is born — her anguish gives place to rapturous joy and the pain is forgotten. [22]You have sorrow now, but I will see you again and then you will rejoice; and no one can rob you of that joy. [23]At that time you won't need to ask me for anything, for you can go directly to the Father and ask him, and he will give you what you ask for because you use my name. [24]You haven't tried this before, [but begin now]. Ask, using my name, and you will receive, and your cup of joy will overflow.

"I Have Overcome the World"

[25]"I have spoken of these matters very guardedly, but the time will come when this will not be necessary and I will tell you plainly all about the Father. [26]Then you will present your petitions over my signature! And I won't need to ask the Father to grant you these requests, [27]for the Father himself loves you dearly because you love me and believe that I came from the Father. [28]Yes, I came from the Father into the world and will leave the world and return to the Father."

[29]"At last you are speaking plainly," his disciples said, "and not in riddles. [30]Now we understand that you know everything and don't need anyone to tell you anything. From this we believe that you came from God."

[31]"Do you finally believe this?" Jesus asked. [32]"But the time is coming — in fact, it is here — when you will be scattered, each one returning to his own home, leaving me alone. Yet I will not be alone, for the Father is with me. [33]I have told you all this so that you will have peace of heart and mind. Here on earth you will have many trials and sorrows; but cheer up, for I have overcome the world."

Chapter 29

JOHN 17

Jesus Prays for Himself and His Followers

[1]When Jesus had finished saying all these things he looked up to heaven and said, "Father, the time has come. Reveal the glory of your Son so that he can give the glory back to you. [2]For you have given him authority over every man and woman in all the earth. He gives eternal life to each one you have given him. [3]And this is the way to have eternal life — by knowing you, the only true God, and Jesus Christ, the one you sent to earth! [4]I brought glory to you here on earth by doing everything you told me to. [5]And now, Father, reveal my glory as I stand in your presence, the glory we shared before the world began.

[6]"I have told these men all about you. They were in the world, but then you gave them to me. Actually, they were always yours, and you gave them to me; and they have obeyed you. [7]Now they know that everything I have is a gift from you, [8]for I have passed on to them the commands you gave me; and they accepted them and know that I came down to earth from you, and they believe you sent me.

[9]"My plea is not for the world but for those you have given me because they belong to you. [10]And all of them, since they are mine, belong to you; and you have given them back to me with everything else of yours, and so *they are my glory!* [11]Now I am leaving the world, and leaving them be-

hind, and coming to you. Holy Father, keep them in your own care — all those you have given me — so that they will be united just as we are, with none missing. [12]During my time here I have kept safe within your family all these you gave me. I guarded them so that not one perished, except the son of hell, as the Scriptures foretold.

[13]"And now I am coming to you. I have told them many things while I was with them so that they would be filled with my joy. [14]I have given them your commands. And the world hates them because they don't fit in with it, just as I don't. [15]I'm not asking you to take them out of the world, but to keep them safe from Satan's power. [16]They are not part of this world any more than I am. [17]Make them pure and holy through teaching them your words of truth. [18]As you sent me into the world, I am sending them into the world, [19]and I consecrate myself to meet their need for growth in truth in holiness.

[20]"I am not praying for these alone but also for the future believers who will come to me because of the testimony of these. [21]My prayer for all of them is that they will be of one heart and mind, just as you and I are, Father — that just as you are in me and I am in you, so they will be in us, and the world will believe you sent me.

[22]"I have given them the glory you gave me — the glorious unity of being one, as we are — [23]I in them and you in me, all being perfected into one — so that the world will know you sent me and will understand that you love them as much as you love me. [24]Father, I want them with me — these you've given me — so that they can see my glory. You gave me the glory because you loved me before the world began!

[25]"O righteous Father, the world doesn't know you, but I do; and these disciples know you sent me. [26]And I have

revealed you to them, and will keep on revealing you so that the mighty love you have for me may be in them, and I in them."

Chapter 30

Jesus in Gethsemane

³⁶Then Jesus brought them to a garden grove, Gethsemane, and told them to sit down and wait while he went on ahead to pray. ³⁷He took Peter with him and Zebedee's two sons James and John, and began to be filled with anguish and despair.

³⁸Then he told them, "My soul is crushed with horror and sadness to the point of death . . . stay here . . . stay awake with me."

³⁹He went forward a little, and fell face downward on the ground, and prayed, "My Father! If it is possible, let this cup be taken away from me. But I want your will, not mine."

⁴⁰Then he returned to the three disciples and found them asleep. "Peter," he called, "couldn't you even stay awake with me one hour? ⁴¹Keep alert and pray. Otherwise temptation will overpower you. For the spirit indeed is willing, but how weak the body is!"

⁴²Again he left them and prayed, "My Father! If this cup cannot go away until I drink it all, your will be done."

⁴³He returned to them again and found them sleeping, for their eyes were heavy, ⁴⁴so he went back to prayer the third time, saying the same things again.

⁴⁵Then he came to the disciples and said, "Sleep on now and take your rest . . . but no! The time has come! I am

betrayed into the hands of evil men! ⁴⁶Up! Let's be going! Look! Here comes the man who is betraying me!"

Jesus Betrayed and Arrested

⁴⁷At that very moment while he was still speaking, Judas, one of the Twelve, arrived with a great crowd armed with swords and clubs, sent by the Jewish leaders. ⁴⁸Judas had told them to arrest the man he greeted, for that would be the one they were after. ⁴⁹So now Judas came straight to Jesus and said, "Hello, Master!" and embraced him in a friendly fashion. ⁵⁰Jesus said, "My friend, go ahead and do what you have come for."...

JOHN 18

^{4,5}Jesus fully realized all that was going to happen to him. Stepping forward to meet them he asked, "Whom are you looking for?"

"Jesus of Nazareth," they replied.

"I am he," Jesus said. ⁶And as he said it, they all fell backwards to the ground!

⁷Once more he asked them, "Whom are you searching for?"

And again they replied, "Jesus of Nazareth."

⁸"I told you I am he," Jesus said; "and since I am the one you are after, let these others go." ⁹He did this to carry out the prophecy he had just made, "I have not lost a single one of those you gave me . . . . "

¹⁰Then Simon Peter drew a sword and slashed off the right ear of Malchus, the High Priest's servant.

LUKE 22

⁵¹But Jesus said, "Don't resist anymore." And he touched the place where the man's ear had been and restored it.

JOHN 18

[11]{Then} ...Jesus said to Peter, "Put your sword away. shall I not drink from the cup the Father has given me?"

MATT. 26

[52]{Jesus continued,} ..."Those using swords will get killed. [53]Don't you realize that I could ask my Father for thousands of angels to protect us, and he would send them instantly? [54]But if I did, how would the Scriptures be fulfilled that describe what is happening now?" [55]Then Jesus spoke to the crowd. "Am I some dangerous criminal," he asked, "that you had to arm yourselves with swords and clubs before you could arrest me? I was with you teaching daily in the Temple and you didn't stop me then. [56]But this is all happening to fulfill the words of the prophets as recorded in the Scriptures."

At that point, all the disciples deserted him and fled.

MARK 14

A Young Man Flees from the Mob

[51,52]There was, however, a young man following along behind, clothed only in a linen nightshirt. When the mob tried to grab him, he escaped, though his clothes were torn off in the process, so that he ran away completely naked.

JOHN 18

Jesus is Taken to Annas

[12]So the Jewish police, with the soldiers and their lieutenant, arrested Jesus and tied him. [13]First they took him to Annas, the father-in-law of Caiaphas, the High Priest that year. [14]Caiaphas was the one who told the other Jewish leaders, "Better that one should die for all."

[15]Simon Peter followed along behind, as did another of the disciples who was acquainted with the High Priest. So

that other disciple was permitted into the courtyard along with Jesus, [16]while Peter stood outside the gate. Then the other disciple spoke to the girl watching at the gate, and she let Peter in.

JOHN 18

Annas Questions Jesus

[19]Inside, the High Priest began asking Jesus about his followers and what he had been teaching them.

[20]Jesus replied, "What I teach is widely known, for I have preached regularly in the synagogue and Temple; I have been heard by all the Jewish leaders and teach nothing in private that I have not said in public. [21]Why are you asking me this question? Ask those who heard me. You have some of them here. They know what I said."

[22]One of the soldiers standing there struck Jesus with his fist. "Is that the way to answer the High Priest?" he demanded.

[23]"If I lied, prove it," Jesus replied. "Should you hit a man for telling the truth?"

[24]Then Annas sent Jesus, bound, to Caiaphas the High Priest.

MARK 14

Jesus Before Caiaphas and the Jewish Court

[53]Jesus was led to the High Priest's home where all of the chief priests and other Jewish leaders soon gathered.

MARK 14

[55]Inside, the chief priests and the whole Jewish Supreme Court were trying to find something against Jesus that would be sufficient to condemn him to death. But there efforts were in vain. [56]Many false winesses volunteered, but they contradicted each other.

⁵⁷Finally some men stood up to lie about him and said, ⁵⁸"We heard him say, 'I will destroy this Temple made with human hands and in three days I will build another, made without human hands!' " ⁵⁹But even then they didn't get their stories straight!

⁶⁰Then the High Priest stood up before the Court and asked Jesus, "Do you refuse to answer this charge? What do you have to say for yourself?"

⁶¹To this Jesus made no reply.

Then the High Priest asked him. "Are you the Messiah, the Son of God?"

⁶²Jesus said, "I am, and you will see me sitting at the right hand of God, and returning to earth in the clouds of heaven."

MATT. 26

⁶⁵,⁶⁶Then the High Priest tore at his own clothing, shouting, "Blasphemy! What need have we for other witnesses? You have all heard him say it! What is your verdict?"

They shouted, "Death! — Death! — Death!"

⁶⁷Then they spat in his face and struck him and some slapped him, ⁶⁸saying, "Prophesy to us, you Messiah! Who struck you that time?"

LUKE 22

⁶⁵And they threw all sorts of other insults at him.

MARK 14

Peter's Three Denials

⁶⁶,⁶⁷Meanwhile Peter was below in the courtyard. One of the maids who worked for the High Priest noticed Peter warming himself at the fire.

She looked at him closely and then announced, *"You were with Jesus, the Nazarene."*

[68]Peter denied it. "I don't know what you're talking about!" he said, and walked over to the edge of the courtyard.

Just then, a rooster crowed.

[69]The maid saw him standing there and began telling others, "There he is! There's that disciple of Jesus!"

[70]Peter denied it again.

A little later others standing around the fire began saying to Peter, "You are, too, one of them, for you are from Galilee!"

[71]He began to curse and swear. "I don't even know this fellow you are talking about," he said.

[72]And immediately the rooster crowed the second time. Suddenly Jesus' words flashed through Peter's mind: "Before the cock crows twice, you will deny me three times." And he began to cry.

LUKE 22

Jesus Before the Jewish Court

[66]Early the next morning at daybreak the Jewish Supreme Court assembled, including the chief priests and all the top religious authorities of the nation. Jesus was led before this Council, [67,68]and instructed to state whether or not he claimed to be the Messiah.

But he replied, "If I tell you, you won't believe me or let me present my case. [69]But the time is soon coming when I, the Messiah, shall be enthroned beside almighty God."

[70]They all shouted, "Then you claim you are the Son of God?"

And he replied, "Yes, I am."

[71]"What need do we have for further witnesses?" they shouted. "For we ourselves have heard him say it."

MATT. 27

Judas Commits Suicide

³About that time Judas, who betrayed him, when he saw that Jesus had been condemned to die, changed his mind and deeply regretted what he had done, and brought back the money to the chief priests and other Jewish leaders.

⁴"I have sinned," he declared, "for I have betrayed an innocent man."

"That's your problem," they retorted.

⁵Then he threw the money onto the floor of the Temple and went out and hanged himself. ⁶The chief priests picked the money up. "We can't put it in the collection," they said, "since it's against our laws to accept money paid for murder."

⁷They talked it over and finally decided to buy a certain field where the clay was used by potters, and to make it into a cemetery for foreigners who died in Jerusalem. ⁸That is why the cemetery is still called "The Field of Blood."

⁹This fulfilled the prophecy of Jeremiah which says,

"They took the thirty pieces of silver — the price at which he was valued by the people of Israel — ¹⁰and purchased a field from the potters as the Lord directed me."

Chapter 31

JOHN 18

Jesus is Taken to Pilate

²⁸Jesus' trial before Caiaphas ended in the early hours of the morning. Next he was taken to the palace of the Roman governor. His accusers wouldn't go in themselves for that would "defile" them, they said, and they wouldn't be allowed to eat the Passover lamb. ²⁹So Pilate, the governor, went out to them and asked, "What is your charge against this man? "What are you accusing him of doing?"

³⁰"We wouldn't have arrested him if he weren't a criminal!" they retorted,

³¹"Then take him away and judge him yourselves by your own laws," Pilate told them.

"But we want him crucified," they demanded, and your approval is required." ³²This fulfilled Jesus' prediction concerning the method of his execution.

³³Then Pilate went back into the palace and called for Jesus to be brought to him. "Are you the King of the Jews?" he asked him.

³⁴" 'King' as *you* use the word or as the *Jews* use it?" Jesus asked.

³⁵"Am I a Jew?" Pilate retorted. "Your own people and their chief priests brought you here. Why? What have you done?"

³⁶Then Jesus answered, "I am not an earthly king. If I were, my followers would have fought when I was arrested by the Jewish leaders. But my Kingdom is not of the world."

³⁷Pilate replied, "But you are a king then?"

"Yes," Jesus said. "I was born for that purpose. And I came to bring truth to the world. All who love the truth are my followers."

³⁸"What is truth?" Pilate exclaimed. Then he went out again to the people and told them, "He is not guilty of any crime."

LUKE 23

⁵Then they became desperate. "But he is causing riots against the government everywhere he goes, all over Judea, from Galilee to Jerusalem

Pilate Sends Jesus to Herod

⁶"Is he then a Galilean?" Pilate asked.

⁷When they told him yes, Pilate said to take him to King Herod, for Galilee was under Herod's jurisdiction; and Herod happened to be in Jerusalem at the time. ⁸Herod was delighted at the opportunity to see Jesus, for he had heard a lot about him and had been hoping to see him perform a miracle. ⁹He asked Jesus question after question, but there was no reply. ¹⁰Meanwhile, the chief priests and the other religious leaders stood there shouting their accusations.

¹¹Now Herod and soldiers began mocking and ridiculing Jesus; and putting a kingly robe on him, they sent him back to Pilate. ¹²That day Herod and Pilate — enemies before — became fast friends.

¹³Then Pilate called together the chief priests and other Jewish leaders, along with the people, ¹⁴and announced his veredict:

"You brought this man to me, accusing him of leading a revolt against the Roman government. I have examined him thoroughly on this point and find him innocent. [15]Herod came to the same conclusion and sent him back to us — nothing this man has done calls for the death penalty. [16]I will therefore have him scourged with leaded thongs and release him.

MATT. 27

The Crowds Demand Jesus' Death

[15]Now the governor's custom was to release one Jewish prisoner each year during the Passover celebration — anyone they wanted. [16]This year there was a particularly notorious criminal in jail named Barabbas, [17]and as the crowds gathered before Pilate's house that morning he asked them, "Which shall I release to you — Barabbas, or Jesus your Messiah?" [18]For he knew very well that the Jewish leaders had arrested Jesus out of envy because of his popularity with the people.

[19]Just then, as he was presiding over the court, Pilate's wife sent him this message: "Leave this good man alone; for I had a terrible nightmare concerning him last night."

[20]Meanwhile the chief priests and Jewish officials persuaded the crowds to ask for Barabbas' release, and for Jesus' death. [21]So when the governor asked again, "Which of these two shall I release to you?" the crowd shouted back their reply: "Barabbas!"

[22]"Then what shall I do with Jesus, your Messiah?" Pilate asked.

And they shouted, "Crucify him!"

[23]"Why?" Pilate demanded. "What has he done wrong?" But they kept shouting, "Crucify! Crucify!"

[24]When Pilate saw that he wasn't getting anywhere, and that a riot was developing, he sent for a bowl of water and

washed his hands before the crowd, saying, "I am innocent of the blood of this good man!" The responsibility is yours!"

²⁵And the mob yelled back, "His blood be on us and on our children!"

²⁶Then Pilate released Barabbas to them...

JOHN 19

¹Then {he} laid open Jesus' back with a leaded whip...

MARK 15

¹⁶,¹⁷{And} ...the Roman soldiers took him into the barracks of the palace, called out the entire palace guard, dressed him in a purple robe, and made a crown of long, sharp thorns and put it on his head. ¹⁸Then they saluted him, yelling, "Yea! King of the Jews!" ¹⁹And they beat him on the head with a cane, and spat on him and went down on their knees to "worship" him.

JOHN 19

Jesus is Sentenced to Death

⁴Pilate went outside again and said to the Jews, "I am going to bring him out to you now, but understand clearly that I find him *not guilty.*"

⁵Then Jesus came out wearing the crown of thorns and the purple robe. And Pilate said, "Behold the man!"

⁶At the sight of him the chief priests and Jewish officials began yelling, "Crucify! Crucify!"

"*You* crucify him," Pilate said. "I find him *not guilty.*"

⁷They replied, "By our laws he ought to die because he called himself the Son of God."

⁸When Pilate heard this, he was more frightened than ever. ⁹He took Jesus back into the palace again and asked him, "Where are you from?" but Jesus gave no answer.

[10]"You won't talk to me?" Pilate demanded. "Don't you realize that I have the power to release you or to crucify you?"

[11]Then Jesus said, "You would have no power at all over me unless it were given to you from above. So those who brought me to you have the greater sin."

[12]Then Pilate tried to release him, but the Jewish leaders told him, "If you release this man, you are no friend of Caesar's. Anyone who declares himself a king is a rebel against Caesar."

[13]At these words Pilate brought Jesus out to them again and sat down at the judgement bench on the stone-paved platform. [14]It was now about noon of the day before Passover.

And Pilate said to the Jews, "Here is your king!"

[15]"Away with him," they yelled. "Away with him — crucify him!"

"What? Crucify your king?" Pilate asked.

"We have no king but Caesar," the chief priests shouted back.

[16]Then Pilate gave Jesus to them to be crucified.

MARK 15

[20]{Then} ...they took off the purple robe and put his own clothes on him again, and led him away to be crucified.

LUKE 23

The Crucifixion

[26]As the crowd led Jesus away to his death, Simon of Cyrene, who was just coming into Jerusalem from the country, was forced to follow, carrying Jesus' cross. [27]Great crowds trailed along behind, and many grief-stricken women.

²⁸But Jesus turned and said to them, "Daughters of Jerusalem, don't weep for me, but for yourselves and for your children. ²⁹For the days are coming when the women who have no children will be counted fortunate indeed. ³⁰Mankind will beg the mountains to fall on them and crush them, and the hills to to bury them. ³¹For if such things as this are done to me, the Living Tree, what will they do to you?"

³²,³³Two others, criminals, were led out to be executed with him at a place called "The Skull." There all three were crucified — Jesus on the center cross, and the two criminals on either side.

³⁴"Father, forgive these people," Jesus said, "for they don't know what they are doing."...

JOHN 19

Pilate Names Jesus King of the Jews

¹⁹And Pilate posted a sign over him reading, "Jesus of Nazareth, the King of the Jews." ²⁰The place where Jesus was crucified was near the city; and the signboard was written in Hebrew, Latin, and Greek, so that many people read it.

²¹Then the chief priests said to Pilate, "Change it from 'The King of the Jews' to '*He said,* I am the King of the Jews.' "

²²Pilate repied, "What I have written, I have written. It stays exactly as it is."

The Soldiers Throw Dice for His Robe

²³,²⁴When the soldiers crucified Jesus, they put his garments into four piles, one for each of them. But they said, "Let's not tear up his robe," for it was seamless. "Let's throw dice to see who gets it. This fulfilled the Scripture that says,

"They divided my clothes among them, and cast lots for my robe."

[25]So that is what they did...

MARK 15

[27]Two robbers were also crucified that morning, their crosses on either side of his. [28]And so the Scripture was fulfilled that said, "He was counted among evil men."

MATT. 27

[39]And the people passing by hurled abuse, shaking their heads at him and saying, [40]"So! You can destroy the Temple and build it again in three days, can you? Well, then, come on down from the cross if you are the Son of God!"

[41,42,43]And the chief priests and Jewish leaders also mocked him. "He saved others," they scoffed, "but he can't save himself! So you are the King of Israel, are you? Come down from the cross and we'll believe you! He trusted God — let God show his approval by delivering him! Didn't he say, 'I am God's Son'?"

LUKE 23

The Two Criminals

[39]One of the criminals hanging beside him scoffed, "So you're the Messiah, are you? Prove it by saving yourself — and us, too, while you're at it!"

[40,41]But the other criminal protested. "Don't you even fear God when you are dying? We deserve to die for our evil deeds, but this man hasn't done one thing wrong." [42]Then he said, "Jesus, remember me when you come into your Kingdom."

[43]And Jesus replied, "Today you will be with me in Paradise. This is a solemn promise."

JOHN 19

²⁵…Standing near the cross were Jesus' mother, Mary, his aunt, the wife of Cleopas, and Mary Magdalene. ²⁶When Jesus saw his mother standing there beside me {John}, his close friend, he said to her, "He is your son,"

²⁷And to me he said, "She is your mother!" And from then I took her into my home.

MARK 15

³³About noon, darkness fell across the entire land, lasting until three o' clock that afternoon.

³⁴Then Jesus called out with a loud voice, "Eli, Eli, lama sabacthani?" ("My God, my God, why have you deserted me?")

³⁵Some of the people standing there thought he was calling for the prophet Elijah. ³⁶So one man ran and got a sponge and filled it with sour wine and held it up to him on a stick.

JOHN 19

²⁸Jesus knew that everything was now finished, and to fulfill the Scriptures said, "I'm thirsty."

JOHN 19

³⁰When Jesus had tasted it, he said, "It is finished,"…

LUKE 23

⁴⁶Then Jesus shouted, "Father, I commit my spirit to you," and with those words he died.

MARK 15

³⁹When the Roman officer standing beside his cross saw how he dismissed his spirit, he exclaimed, "Truly, this was the Son of God!"

MATT. 27

The Temple Curtain Splits Apart

[51]And look! The curtain secluding the Holiest Place in the Temple was split apart from top to bottom; and the earth shook, and rocks broke, [52]and tombs opened, and many godly men and women who had died came back to life again. [53]After Jesus' resurrection, they left the cemetery and went into Jerusalem, and appeared to many people there.

MATT. 27

[55]And many women who had come down from Galilee with Jesus to care for him were watching from a distance. [56]Among them were Mary Magdalene and Mary the mother of James and Joseph, and the mother of James and John (the sons of Zebedee).

JOHN 19

Blood and Water Flow from Jesus' Side

[31]The Jewish leaders didn't want the victims hanging there the next day, which was the Sabbath (and a very special Sabbath at that, for it was the Passover), so they asked Pilate to order the legs of the men broken to hasten death; then their bodies could be taken down. [32]So the soldiers came and broke the legs of the two men crucified with Jesus; [33]but when they came to him, they saw that he was dead already, so they didn't break his. [34]However, one of the soldiers pierced his side with a spear, and blood and water flowed out. [35]I {John} saw all this myself and have given an accurate report so that you also can believe. [36,37]The soldiers did this in fulfillment of the Scripture that says, "Not one of his bones shall be broken," and "They shall look on him whom they pierced."

Chapter 32

Jesus Laid in the Tomb

[42,43]This all happened the day before the Sabbath. Late that afternoon Joseph from Arimathea, an honored member of the Jewish Supreme Court (who personally was eagerly expecting the arrival of God's Kingdom), gathered his courage and went to Pilate and asked for Jesus' body.

[44]Pilate couldn't believe that Jesus was already dead so he called for the Roman officer in charge and asked him. [45]The officer confirmed the fact, and Pilate told Joseph he could have the body.

[46]Joseph bought a long sheet of linen cloth and, taking Jesus' body down from the cross, wound it in the cloth and laid it in a rock-hewn tomb, and rolled a stone in front of the entrance.

[47](Mary Magdalene and Mary the mother of Joses were watching as Jesus was laid away.)

MATT. 27

Guards are Posted at the Tomb

[62]The next day—at the close of the first day of the Passover ceremonies—the chief priests and Pharisees went to Pilate, [63]and told him, "Sir, that liar once said, 'After three days I will come back to life again.' [64]So we request an order from you sealing the tomb until the third day, to prevent his

disciples from coming and stealing his body and then telling everyone he came back to life! If that happens we'll be worse off than we were at first."

⁶⁵"Use your own Temple police," Pilate told them. "They can guard it safely enough."

⁶⁶So they sealed the stone and posted guards to protect it from intrusion.

MARK 16

Jesus Rises from the Dead

¹The next evening, when the Sabbath ended, Mary Magdalene and Salome and Mary the mother of James went out and purchased embalming spices.

Early the next morning, just at sunrise, they carried them out to the tomb. ³On the way they were discussing how they could ever roll aside the huge stone from the entrance.

MATT. 28

²Suddenly there was a great earthquake; for an angel of the Lord came down from heaven and rolled aside the stone and sat on it. ³His face shone like lightning and his clothing was a brilliant white. ⁴The guards shook with fear when they saw him, and fell into a dead faint.

⁵Then the angel spoke to the women. "Don't be frightened!" he said. "I know you are looking for Jesus, who was crucified, ⁶but he isn't here! For he has come back to life again, just as he said he would. Come in and see where his body was lying. . . .

MARK 16

⁷"Now go and give this message to his disciples including Peter:

" 'Jesus is going ahead of you to Galilee. You will see him there, just as he told you before he died!' "

[8]The women fled from the tomb, trembling and bewildered, too frightened to talk.

JOHN 20

[2]{Then they} ...ran and found Simon Peter and me {John} and said, "They have taken the Lord's body out of the tomb, and I don't know where they have put him!"

[3,4]We ran to the tomb to see; I outran Peter and got there first, [5]and stooped and looked in and saw the linen cloth lying there, but I didn't go in. [6]Then Simon Peter arrived and went on inside. He also noticed the cloth lying there, [7]while the swath that had covered Jesus' head was rolled up in a bundle and was lying at the side. [8]Then I went in too, and saw, and believed [that he had risen] — [9]for until then we hadn't realized that the Scriptures said he would come to life again!

Mary Sees the Risen Jesus

[10]We went on home, [11]and by that time Mary had returned to the tomb and was standing outside crying. And as she wept, she stooped and looked in [12]and saw two white-robed angels sitting at the head and foot of the place where the body of Jesus had been lying.

[13]"Why are you crying?" the angels asked her.

"Because they have taken away my Lord," she replied, "and I don't know where they have put him."

[14]She glanced over her shoulder and saw someone standing behind her. It was Jesus, but she didn't recognize him!

[15]"Why are you crying?" he asked her. "Whom are you looking for?"

She thought he was the gardener. "Sir," she said, "if you have taken him away, tell me where you have put him, and I will go and get him."

[16]"Mary!" Jesus said. She turned toward him.

Chapter Thirty-Two

"Master!" she exclaimed.

[17]"Don't touch me," he cautioned, "for I haven't yet ascended to the Father. But go and find my brothers and tell them that I ascend to my Father and your Father, my God and your God."

[18]Mary Magdalene found the disciples and told them, "I have seen the Lord!" Then she gave them his message.

MATT. 28

[11]...Some of the Temple police who had been guarding the tomb went to the chief priests and told them what had happened. [12,13]A meeting of all the Jewish leaders was called, and it was decided to bribe the police to say they had all been asleep when Jesus' disciples came during the night and stole his body.

[14]"If the governor hears about it," the Council promised, "we'll stand up for you and everything will be all right."

[15]So the police accepted the bribe and said what they were told to. Their story spread widely among the Jews, and is still believed by them to this very day.

LUKE 24

On the Emmaus Road

[13]That same day, Sunday, two of Jesus' followers were walking to the village of Emmaus, seven miles out of Jerusalem. [14]As they walked along they were talking of Jesus' death, [15]when suddenly Jesus himself came along and joined them and began walking beside them. [16]But they didn't recognize him, for God kept them from it.

[17]"You seem to be in a deep discussion about something," he said. "What are you so concerned about?" They stopped short, sadness written across their faces. [18]And one of them, Cleopas, replied, "You must be the only person in

Jerusalem who hasn't heard about the terrible things that happened there last week."

[19]"What things?" Jesus asked.

"The things that happened to Jesus, the Man from Nazareth," they said. "He was a Prophet who did incredible miracles and was a mighty Teacher, highly regarded by both God and man. [20]But the chief priests and our religious leaders arrested him and handed him over to the Roman government to be condemned to death, and they crucified him. [21]We had thought he was the glorious Messiah and that he had come to rescue Israel.

"And now, besides all this — which happened three days ago — [22,23]some women from our group of his followers were at his tomb early this morning and came back with an amazing report that his body was missing, and that they had seen some angels there who told them Jesus is alive! [24]Some of our men ran out to see, and sure enough, Jesus' body was gone, just as the women had said."

[25]Then Jesus said to them, "You are such foolish, foolish people! You find it so hard to believe all that the prophets wrote in the Scriptures! [26]Wasn't it clearly predicted by the prophets that the Messiah would have to suffer all these things before entering his time of glory?"

[27]Then Jesus quoted them passage after passage from the writings of the prophets, beginning with the book of Genesis and going right on through the Scriptures, explaining what the passages meant and what they said about himself.

[28]By this time they were nearing Emmaus and the end of their journey. Jesus would have gone on, [29]but they begged him to stay the night with them, as it was getting late. So he went home with them. [30]As they sat down to eat, he asked God's blessing on the food and then took a small

loaf of bread and broke it and was passing it over to them, [31]when suddenly—it was as though their eyes were opened—they recognized him! And at that moment he disappeared!

[32]They began telling each other how their hearts had felt strangely warm as he talked with them and explained the Scriptures during the walk down the road. [33,34]Within the hour they were on their way back to Jerusalem, where the eleven disciples and the other followers of Jesus greeted them with these words, "The Lord has really risen! He appeared to Peter!"

[35]Then the two from Emmaus told their story of how Jesus had appeared to them as they were walking along the road and how they had recognized him as he was breaking the bread.

JOHN 20

Jesus Appears Among His Disciples

[19]That evening the disciples were meeting behind locked doors, in fear of the Jewish leaders, when suddenly Jesus was standing there among them! After greeting them, [20]he showed them his hands and side. And how wonderful was their joy as they saw their Lord!

[21]He spoke to them again and said, "As the Father has sent me, even so I am sending you." [22]Then he breathed on them and told them, "Receive the Holy Spirit. [23]If you forgive anyone's sins, they are forgiven. If you refuse to forgive them, they are unforgiven."

Thomas' Unbelief

[24]One of the disciples, Thomas, "The Twin," was not there at the time with the others. [25]When they kept telling him, "We have seen the Lord," he replied, "I won't believe

it unless I see the nail wounds in his hands — and put my fingers into them — and place my hand into his side."

²⁶Eight days later the disciples were together again, and this time Thomas was with them. The doors were locked; but suddenly, as before, Jesus was standing among them and greeting them.

²⁷Then he said to Thomas, "Put your finger into my hands. Put your hand into my side. Don't be faithless any longer. Believe!"

²⁸"My Lord and my God!" Thomas said.

²⁹Then Jesus told him, "You believe because you have seen me. But blessed are those who haven't seen me and believe anyway."

JOHN 21

Jesus Appears to Seven of His Disciples

¹Later Jesus appeared again to the disciples beside the Lake of Galilee. This is how it happened:

²A group of us were there — Simon Peter, Thomas, "The Twin," Nathaniel from Cana in Galilee, my {John's} brother James and I and two other disciples.

³Simon Peter said, "I'm going fishing."

"We'll come too," we all said. We did, but caught nothing all night.

⁴At dawn we saw a man standing on the beach but couldn't see who he was.

⁵He called, "Any fish, boys?"

"No," we replied.

⁶Then he said, "Throw out your net on the right-hand side of the boat, and you'll get plenty of them!" So we did, and couldn't draw in the net because of the weight of the fish, there were so many!

⁷Then I said to Peter, "It is the Lord!" At that, Simon Peter put on his tunic (for he was stripped to the waist) and

jumped into the water [and swam ashore]. [8]The rest of us stayed in the boat and pulled the loaded net to the beach, about 300 feet away. [9]When we got there, we saw that a fire was kindled and fish were frying over it, and there was bread.

[10]"Bring some of the fish you've just caught," Jesus said. [11]So Simon Peter went out and dragged the net ashore. By his count there were 153 large fish; and yet the net hadn't torn.

[12]"Now come and have some breakfast!" Jesus said; and none of us dared ask him if he really was the Lord, for we were quite sure of it. [13]Then Jesus went around serving us the bread and fish.

[14]This was the third time Jesus had appeared to us since his return from the dead.

Take Care of My Sheep

[15]After breakfast Jesus said to Simon Peter, "Simon, son of John, do you love me more than these others?"

"Yes," Peter replied, "You know I am your friend."

"Then feed my lambs," Jesus told him.

[16]Jesus repeated the question: "Simon, son of John, do you *really* love me?"

"Yes, Lord," Peter said, "you know I am your friend."

"Then take care of my sheep," Jesus said.

[17]Once more he asked him, "Simon, son of John, are you even my friend?"

Peter was grieved at the way Jesus asked the question this third time. "Lord, you know my heart; you know I am," he said.

Jesus said, "Then feed my little sheep. [18]When you were young, you were able to do as you liked and go wherever you wanted to; but when you are old, you will stretch out your hands and others will direct you and take you where you don't want go." [19]Jesus said this to let him know what kind of death he would die to glorify God. Then Jesus told him, "Follow me."

The Disciple Jesus Loved

[20]Peter turned around and saw the disciple Jesus loved following, the one who had leaned around at supper that time to ask Jesus, "Master, which of us will betray you?" [21]Peter asked Jesus, "What about him, Lord? What sort of death will he die?"

[22]Jesus replied, "If I want him to live until I return, what is that to you? *You* follow me."

[23]So the rumor spread among the brotherhood that that disciple wouldn't die! But that isn't what Jesus said at all! He only said, "If I want him to live until I come, what is that to you?"

[24]*I am that disciple!* I {John} saw these events and have recorded them here. And we all know that my account of these things is accurate.

Chapter 33

Go and Make Disciples

¹⁶Then the eleven disciples left for Galilee, going to the mountain where Jesus had said they would find him. ¹⁷There they met him and worshiped him—but some of them weren't sure it really was Jesus!

¹⁸He told his disciples, "I have been given all authority in heaven and earth. ¹⁹Therefore go and make disciples in all the nations, baptizing them into the name of the Father and of the Son and of the Holy Spirit...

MARK 16

Believe and Use My Authority

¹⁶"Those who believe and are baptized will be saved. But those who refuse to believe will be condemned.

¹⁷"And those who believe shall use my authority to cast out demons, and they shall speak in new tongues. ¹⁸They will be able even to handle snakes with safety, and if they drink anything poisonous, it won't hurt them; and they will be able to place their hands on the sick and heal them.

MATT. 28

²⁰"...Teach these new disciples to obey all the commands I have given you; and be sure of this—that I am with you always, even to the end of the world."

LUKE 24

⁴⁴Then he said, "When I was with you before, don't you remember my telling you that everything written about me by Moses and the prophets and in the Psalms must all come true?" ⁴⁵Then he opened their minds to understand at last these many Scriptures! ⁴⁶And he said, "Yes, it was written long ago that the Messiah must suffer and die and rise again from the dead on the third day; ⁴⁷and that this message of salvation should be taken from Jerusalem to all the nations: *There is forgiveness of sins for all who turn to me.* ⁴⁸You have seen these prophecies come true.

⁴⁹"And now I will send the Holy Spirit upon you, just as my Father promised. Don't begin telling others yet — stay here in the city until the Holy Spirit comes and fills you with power from heaven."

Jesus Ascends to Heaven

⁵⁰Then Jesus led them out along the road to Bethany, and lifting his hands to heaven, he blessed them, ⁵¹and then began rising into the sky, and went on to heaven. ⁵²And they worshiped him, and returned to Jerusalem filled with mighty joy, ⁵³and were continually in the Temple, praising God.

JOHN 20

The Reason for Writing These Things

³⁰,³¹Jesus' disciples saw him do many other miracles besides the ones told about in this book, but these are recorded so that you will believe that he is the Messiah, the Son of God, and that believing in him you will have life.

JOHN 21

[25]And I suppose that if all the other events in Jesus' life were written, the whole world could hardly contain the books!

JOHN 1

[10]But although he made the world, the world didn't recognize him when he came. [11,12]Even in his own land and among his own people, the Jews, he was not accepted. Only a few would welcome and receive him. But to all who received him, he gave the right to become children of God. All they needed to do was to trust him to save them. [13]All those who believe this are reborn! — not a physical rebirth resulting from human passion or plan — but from the will of God.

[14]And Christ became a human being and lived here on earth among us and was full of loving forgiveness and truth. And some of us have seen his glory — the glory of the only Son of the heavenly Father!

[15]John pointed him out to the people, telling the crowds, "This is the one I was talking about when I said, 'Someone is coming who is greater by far than I am — for he existed long before I did!' " [16]We have all benefited from the rich blessings he brought to us — blessing upon blessing heaped upon us! [17]For Moses gave us only the Law with its rigid demands and merciless justice, while Jesus Christ brought us loving forgiveness as well. [18]No one has ever actually seen God, but, of course, his only Son has, for he is the companion of the Father and has told us all about him.

A Plan For Your Life!

If you have never committed your life to Jesus Christ, there is no better time to do so than right now. If you want Him to be your Lord, your Savior and your friend, follow these simple steps:

1. **Acknowledge and Confess Your Sin.**

   Sin is man's greatest problem. It is what separates all of us from God. Romans 3:23 tells us: *"All have sinned and fall short of the glory of God."* The first step in being spiritually born again is to acknowledge before God that we have sinned and that only He can forgive that sin: *"If we confess our sins, He is faithful and just and will forgive us our sins and purify us from all unrighteousness."* (1 John 1:9.)

2. **Invite Christ into Your Life.**

   God loves you, and wants to remove the barrier of sin that separates us from Him. 1 John 4:9,10 reads: *"This is how God showed His love among us: He sent His one and only Son into the world... as an atoning sacrifice for our sins."* Christ paid for our sins with His own life. Now He is asking you to receive Him as your Savior: *"Yet to all who received Him, to those who believed in His name, He gave the right to become children of God."* (John 1:12.)

3. **Be Obedient to Him.**

   Following Christ takes commitment, but when we have invited Him into our lives, we have His strength to call upon. Tell Him that you have turned away from sin (the Bible calls that "repentance"), and that you want Him to help you live as He wants you to. In Matthew 16:24 we read, *"Then Jesus said to His disciples, 'If anyone would come after me, He must deny himself and take up his cross and follow me...'"*

All you need to do, right now, is to pray a simple prayer and talk to God about those three things — confess your sin and ask Him to forgive you, invite Jesus to be the Lord of your life, and ask Him to help you live for Him from now on. You don't need any fancy words; just talk to Him like you would a close friend.

As a new Christian, you will find the help of a good bible-believing local church invaluable. Here you will learn more about God's Word and how to study it. You will also discover the benefits of talking to God in prayer every day. If you need help with any of these things, or if you just need someone to pray with you, the people from whom you received this book would love to hear from you (their address is no doubt clearly stamped or imprinted for your convenience). Of course, you are welcome at any time to call or write to: Philip Cameron Ministries, P.O. Box 241241, Montgomery, AL 36124-1241. Prayer Line: (205) 277-9000.